I0002570

THE THREE ORIGINAL PUBLICATIONS ON VACCINATION AGAINST SMALLPOX

BY

EDWARD JENNER

.

INTRODUCTORY NOTE

EDWARD JENNER *was born at his father's vicarage at Berkeley, Gloucestershire, England, on May 17, 1749. After leaving school, he was apprenticed to a local surgeon, and in 1770 he went to London and became a resident pupil under the great surgeon and anatomist, John Hunter, with whom he remained on intimate terms for the rest of Hunter's life. In 1773 he took up practise at Berkeley, where, except for numerous visits to London, he spent the rest of his life. He died of apoplexy on January 26, 1823.*

Jenner's scientific interests were varied, but the importance of his work in vaccination has overshadowed his other results. Early in his career he had begun to observe the phenomena of cowpox, a disease common in the rural parts of the western counties of England, and he was familiar with the belief, current among the peasantry, that a person who had suffered from the cowpox could not take smallpox. Finally, in 1796, he made his first experiment in vaccination, inoculating a boy of eight with cowpox, and, after his recovery, with smallpox; with the result that the boy did not take the latter disease.

Jenner's first paper on his discovery was never printed; but in 1798 appeared the first of the following treatises. Its reception by the medical profession was highly discouraging; but progress began when Cline, the surgeon of St. Thomas's Hospital, used the treatment with success. Jenner continued his investigations, publishing his results from time to time, and gradually gaining recognition; though opposition to his theory and practise was at first vehement, and has never entirely disappeared. In 1802, Parliament voted him £10,000, and in 1806, £20,000, in recognition of the value of his services, and the sacrifices they had entailed. As early as 1807, Bavaria made vaccination compulsory; and since that date most of the European governments have officially encouraged or compelled the practise; and smallpox has ceased to be the almost universal scourge it was before Jenner's discovery.

150

To

C. H. PARRY, M.D.

AT BATH

MY DEAR FRIEND:

In the present age of scientific investigation it is remarkable that a disease of so peculiar a nature as the cow-pox, which has appeared in this and some of the neighbouring counties for such a series of years, should so long have escaped particular attention. Finding the prevailing notions on the subject, both among men of our profession and others, extremely vague and indeterminate, and conceiving that facts might appear at once both curious and useful, I have instituted as strict an inquiry into the causes and effects of this singular malady as local circumstances would admit.

The following pages are the result, which, from motives of the most affectionate regard, are dedicated to you, by

Your sincere friend,

EDWARD JENNER.

BERKELEY, GLOUCESTERSHIRE,
June 21st, 1798.

VACCINATION
AGAINST SMALLPOX

I

An Inquiry into the Causes and Effects of the Variolæ Vaccinæ, or Cow-Pox. 1798

THE deviation of man from the stage in which he was originally placed by nature seems to have proved to him a prolific source of diseases. From the love of splendour, from the indulgences of luxury, and from his fondness for amusement he has familiarised himself with a great number of animals, which may not originally have been intended for his associates.

The wolf, disarmed of ferocity, is now pillowed in the lady's lap.[1] The cat, the little tiger of our island, whose natural home is the forest, is equally domesticated and caressed. The cow, the hog, the sheep, and the horse, are all, for a variety of purposes, brought under his care and dominion.

There is a disease to which the horse, from his state of domestication, is frequently subject. The farriers have called it the grease. It is an inflammation and swelling in the heel, from which issues matter possessing properties of a very peculiar kind, which seems capable of generating a disease in the human body (after it has undergone the modification which I shall presently speak of), which bears so strong a resemblance to the smallpox that I think it highly probable it may be the source of the disease.

In this dairy country a great number of cows are kept, and the office of milking is performed indiscriminately by

---

[1] The late Mr. John Hunter proved, by experiments, that the dog is the wolf in a degenerate state.

men and maid servants. One of the former having been
appointed to apply dressings to the heels of a horse affected
with the grease, and not paying due attention to cleanliness,
incautiously bears his part in milking the cows, with some
particles of the infectious matter adhering to his fingers.
When this is the case, it commonly happens that a disease
is communicated to the cows, and from the cows to the
dairymaids, which spreads through the farm until the most
of the cattle and domestics feel its unpleasant consequences.
This disease has obtained the name of the cow-pox. It
appears on the nipples of the cows in the form of irregular
pustules. At their first appearance they are commonly of a
palish blue, or rather of a colour somewhat approaching to
livid, and are surrounded by an erysipelatous inflammation.
These pustules, unless a timely remedy be applied, frequently
degenerate into phagedenic ulcers, which prove extremely
troublesome.[2] The animals become indisposed, and the
secretion of milk is much lessened. Inflamed spots now
begin to appear on different parts of the hands of the domestics employed in milking, and sometimes on the wrists,
which quickly run on to suppuration, first assuming the
appearance of the small vesications produced by a burn.
Most commonly they appear about the joints of the fingers
and at their extremities; but whatever parts are affected,
if the situation will admit, these superficial suppurations put
on a circular form, with their edges more elevated than their
centre, and of a colour distantly approaching to blue.
Absorption takes place, and tumours appear in each axilla.
The system becomes affected—the pulse is quickened; and
shiverings, succeeded by heat, with general lassitude and
pains about the loins and limbs, with vomiting, come on.
The head is painful, and the patient is now and then even
affected with delirium. These symptoms, varying in their
degrees of violence, generally continue from one day to
three or four, leaving ulcerated sores about the hands, which,
from the sensibility of the parts, are very troublesome, and
commonly heal slowly, frequently becoming phagedenic, like

[2] They who attend sick cattle in this country find a speedy remedy for
stopping the progress of this complaint in those applications which act chem-
ically upon the morbid matter, such as the solutions of the vitriolum zinci
and the vitriolum cupri, etc.

those from whence they sprung. The lips, nostrils, eyelids, and other parts of the body are sometimes affected with sores; but these evidently arise from their being heedlessly rubbed or scratched with the patient's infected fingers. No eruptions on the skin have followed the decline of the feverish symptoms in any instance that has come under my inspection, one only excepted, and in this case a very few appeared on the arms: they were very minute, of a vivid red colour, and soon died away without advancing to maturation; so that I cannot determine whether they had any connection with the preceding symptoms.

Thus the disease makes its progress from the horse[3] to the nipple of the cow, and from the cow to the human subject.

Morbid matter of various kinds, when absorbed into the system, may produce effects in some degree similar; but what renders the cow-pox virus so extremely singular is that the person who has been thus affected is forever after secure from the infection of the smallpox; neither exposure to the variolous effluvia, nor the insertion of the matter into the skin, producing this distemper.

In support of so extraordinary a fact, I shall lay before my reader a great number of instances.[4]

CASE I.—Joseph Merret, now an under gardener to the Earl of Berkeley, lived as a servant with a farmer near this place in the year 1770, and occasionally assisted in milking his master's cows. Several horses belonging to the farm

[3] Jenner's conclusion that " grease " and cow-pox were the same disease has since been proved erroneous; but this error has not invalidated his main conclusion as to the relation of cow-pox and smallpox.—EDITOR.

[4] It is necessary to observe that pustulous sores frequently appear spontaneously on the nipples of cows, and instances have occurred, though very rarely, of the hands of the servants employed in milking being affected with sores in consequence, and even of their feeling an indisposition from absorption. These pustules are of a much milder nature than those which arise from that contagion which constitutes the true cow-pox. They are always free from the bluish or livid tint so conspicuous in the pustules in that disease. No erysipelas attends them, nor do they shew any phagedenic disposition as in the other case, but quickly terminate in a scab without creating any apparent disorder in the cow. This complaint appears at various seasons of the year, but most commonly in the spring, when the cows are first taken from their winter food and fed with grass. It is very apt to appear also when they are suckling their young. But this disease is not to be considered as similar in any respect to that of which I am treating, as it is incapable of producing any specific effects on the human constitution. However, it is of the greatest consequence to point it out here, lest the want of discrimination should occasion an idea of security from the infection of the smallpox, which might prove delusive.

began to have sore heels, which Merret frequently attended. The cows soon became affected with the cow-pox, and soon after several sores appeared on his hands. Swellings and stiffness in each axilla followed, and he was so much indisposed for several days as to be incapable of pursuing his ordinary employment. Previously to the appearance of the distemper among the cows there was no fresh cow brought into the farm, nor any servant employed who was affected with the cow-pox.

In April, 1795, a general inoculation taking place here, Merret was inoculated with his family; so that a period of twenty-five years had elapsed from his having the cow-pox to this time. However, though the variolous matter was repeatedly inserted into his arm, I found it impracticable to infect him with it; an efflorescence only, taking on an erysipelatous look about the centre, appearing on the skin near the punctured parts. During the whole time that his family had the smallpox, one of whom had it very full, he remained in the house with them, but received no injury from exposure to the contagion.

It is necessary to observe that the utmost care was taken to ascertain, with the most scrupulous precision, that no one whose case is here adduced had gone through the smallpox previous to these attempts to produce that disease.

Had these experiments been conducted in a large city, or in a populous neighbourhood, some doubts might have been entertained; but here, where population is thin, and where such an event as a person's having had the smallpox is always faithfully recorded, no risk of inaccuracy in this particular can arise

CASE II.—Sarah Portlock, of this place, was infected with the cow-pox when a servant at a farmer's in the neighbourhood, twenty-seven years ago.[5]

In the year 1792, conceiving herself, from this circumstance, secure from the infection of the smallpox, she nursed one of her own children who had accidentally caught the

[5] I have purposely selected several cases in which the disease had appeared at a very distant period previous to the experiments made with variolous matter, to shew that the change produced in the constitution is not affected by time.

disease, but no indisposition ensued. During the time she remained in the infected room, variolous matter was inserted into both her arms, but without any further effect than in the preceding case.

CASE III.—John Phillips, a tradesman of this town, had the cow-pox at so early a period as nine years of age. At the age of sixty-two I inoculated him, and was very careful in selecting matter in its most active state. It was taken from the arm of a boy just before the commencement of the eruptive fever, and instantly inserted. It very speedily produced a sting-like feel in the part. An efflorescence appeared, which on the fourth day was rather extensive, and some degree of pain and stiffness were felt about the shoulder; but on the fifth day these symptoms began to disappear, and in a day or two after went entirely off, without producing any effect on the system.

CASE IV.—Mary Barge, of Woodford, in this parish, was inoculated with variolous matter in the year 1791. An efflorescence of a palish red colour soon appeared about the parts where the matter was inserted, and spread itself rather extensively, but died away in a few days without producing any variolous symptoms.[6] She has since been repeatedly employed as a nurse to smallpox patients, without experiencing any ill consequences. This woman had the cow-pox when she lived in the service of a farmer in this parish thirty-one years before.

CASE V.—Mrs. H——, a respectable gentlewoman of this town, had the cow-pox when very young. She received the infection in rather an uncommon manner: it was given by means of her handling some of the same utensils[7] which

[6] It is remarkable that variolous matter, when the system is disposed to reject it, should excite inflammation on the part to which it is applied more speedily than when it produces the smallpox. Indeed, it becomes almost a criterion by which we can determine whether the infection will be received or not. It seems as if a change, which endures through life, had been produced in the action, or disposition to action, in the vessels of the skin; and it is remarkable, too, that whether this change has been effected by the smallpox or the cow-pox that the disposition to sudden cuticular inflammation is the same on the application of variolous matter.

[7] When the cow-pox has prevailed in the dairy, it has often been communicated to those who have not milked the cows, by the handle of the milk pail.

were in use among the servants of the family, who had the disease from milking infected cows. Her hands had many of the cow-pox sores upon them, and they were communicated to her nose, which became inflamed and very much swollen. Soon after this event Mrs. H—— was exposed to the contagion of the smallpox, where it was scarcely possible for her to have escaped, had she been susceptible of it, as she regularly attended a relative who had the disease in so violent a degree that it proved fatal to him.

In the year 1778 the smallpox prevailed very much at Berkeley, and Mrs. H——, not feeling perfectly satisfied respecting her safety (no indisposition having followed her exposure to the smallpox), I inoculated her with active variolous matter. The same appearance followed as in the preceding cases—an efflorescence on the arm without any effect on the constitution.

CASE VI.—It is a fact so well known among our dairy farmers that those who have had the smallpox either escape the cow-pox or are disposed to have it slightly, that as soon as the complaint shews itself among the cattle, assistants are procured, if possible, who are thus rendered less susceptible of it, otherwise the business of the farm could scarcely go forward.

In the month of May, 1796, the cow-pox broke out at Mr. Baker's, a farmer who lives near this place. The disease was communicated by means of a cow which was purchased in an infected state at a neighbouring fair, and not one of the farmer's cows (consisting of thirty) which were at that time milked escaped the contagion. The family consisted of a man servant, two dairymaids, and a servant boy, who, with the farmer himself, were twice a day employed in milking the cattle. The whole of this family, except Sarah Wynne, one of the dairymaids, had gone through the smallpox. The consequence was that the farmer and the servant boy escaped the infection of the cow-pox entirely, and the servant man and one of the maid servants had each of them nothing more then a sore on one of their fingers, which produced no disorder in the system. But the other dairymaid, Sarah Wynné, who never had the smallpox, did not escape in so easy a manner. She caught the complaint from the cows, and was affected with the symptoms described on page 154 in so violent a degree that she was confined to her bed, and rendered incapable for several days of pursuing her ordinary vocations in the farm.

March 28, 1797, I inoculated this girl and carefully rubbed the variolous matter into two slight incisions made upon the left arm. A little inflammation appeared in the usual manner around the parts where the matter was inserted, but so early as the fifth day it vanished entirely without producing any effect on the system.

CASE VII.—Although the preceding history pretty clearly evinces that the constitution is far less susceptible of the contagion of the cow-pox after it has felt that of the smallpox, and although in general, as I have observed, they who have had the smallpox, and are employed in milking cows which are infected with the cow-pox, either escape the disorder, or have sores on the hands without feeling any general indisposition, yet the animal economy is subject to some variation in this respect, which the following relation will point out:

In the summer of the year 1796 the cow-pox appeared at the farm of Mr. Andrews, a considerable dairy adjoining to the town of Berkeley. It was communicated, as in the preceding instance, by an infected cow purchased at a fair in the neighbourhood. The family consisted of the farmer, his wife, two sons, a man and a maid servant; all of whom, except the farmer (who was fearful of the consequences), bore a part in milking the cows. The whole of them, exclusive of the man servant, had regularly gone through the smallpox; but in this case no one who milked the cows escaped the contagion. All of them had sores upon their hands, and some degree of general indisposition, preceded by pains and tumours in the axillæ: but there was no comparison in the severity of the disease as it was felt by the servant man, who had escaped the smallpox, and by those of the family who had not, for, while he was confined to his bed, they were able, without much inconvenience, to follow their ordinary business.

February the 13th, 1797, I availed myself of an opportunity of inoculating William Rodway, the servant man above alluded to.   Variolous matter was inserted into both his arms: in the right, by means of superficial incisions, and into the left by slight punctures into the cutis.   Both were perceptibly inflamed on the third day.   After this the inflammation about the punctures soon died away, but a small appearance of erysipelas was manifest about the edges of the incisions till the eighth day, when a little uneasiness was felt for the space of half an hour in the right axilla. The inflammation then hastily disappeared without producing the most distant mark of affection of the system.

CASE VIII.—Elizabeth Wynne, aged fifty-seven, lived as a servant with a neighbouring farmer thirty-eight years ago. She was then a dairymaid, and the cow-pox broke out among the cows. She caught the disease with the rest of the family, but, compared with them, had it in a very slight degree, one very small sore only breaking out on the little finger of her left hand, and scarcely any perceptible indisposition following it.

As the malady had shewn itself in so slight a manner, and as it had taken place at so distant a period of her life, I was happy with the opportunity of trying the effects of variolous matter upon her constitution, and on the 28th of March, 1797, I inoculated her by making two superficial incisions on the left arm, on which the matter was cautiously rubbed. A little efflorescence soon appeared, and a tingling sensation was felt about the parts where the matter was inserted until the third day, when both began to subside, and so early as the fifth day it was evident that no indisposition would follow.

CASE IX.—Although the cow-pox shields the constitution from the smallpox, and the smallpox proves a protection against its own future poison, yet it appears that the human body is again and again susceptible of the infectious matter of the cow-pox, as the following history will demonstrate.

William Smith, of Pyrton in this parish, contracted this disease when he lived with a neighbouring farmer in the year 1780. One of the horses belonging to the farm had sore heels, and it fell to his lot to attend him. By these means the infection was carried to the cows, and from the cows it was communicated to Smith. On one of his hands were several ulcerated sores, and he was affected with such symptoms as have been before described.

In the year 1791 the cow-pox broke out at another farm where he then lived as a servant, and he became affected with it a second time; and in the year 1794 he was so unfortunate as to catch it again. The disease was equally as severe the second and third time as it was on the first.[a]

In the spring of the year 1795 he was twice inoculated, but no affection of the system could be produced from the variolous matter; and he has since associated with those who had the smallpox in its most contagious state without feeling any effect from it.

CASE X.—Simon Nichols lived as a servant with Mr. Bromedge, a gentleman who resides on his own farm in this parish, in the year 1782. He was employed in applying dressings to the sore heels of one of his master's horses, and at the same time assisted in milking the cows. The cows became affected in consequence, but the disease did not shew itself on their nipples till several weeks after he had begun to dress the horse. He quitted Mr. Bromedge's service, and went to another farm without any sores upon him; but here his hands soon began to be affected in the common way, and he was much indisposed with the usual symptoms. Concealing the nature of the malady from Mr. Cole, his new master, and being there also employed in milking, the cow-pox was communicated to the cows.

Some years afterward Nichols was employed in a farm where the smallpox broke out, when I inoculated him with several other patients, with whom he continued during the whole time of their confinement. His arm inflamed, but neither the inflammation nor his associating with the in-oculated family produced the least effect upon his constitution.

---

[a] This is not the case in general—a second attack is commonly very slight, and so, I am informed, it is among the cows.

CASE XI.—William Stinchcomb was a fellow servant with Nichols at Mr. Bromedge's farm at the time the cattle had the cow-pox, and he was, unfortunately, infected by them. His left hand was very severely affected with several corroding ulcers, and a tumour of considerable size appeared in the axilla of that side. His right hand had only one small tumour upon it, and no sore discovered itself in the corresponding axilla.

In the year 1792 Stinchcomb was inoculated with variolous matter, but no consequences ensued beyond a little inflammation in the arm for a few days. A large party were inoculated at the same time, some of whom had the disease in a more violent degree than is commonly seen from inoculation. He purposely associated with them, but could not receive the smallpox.

During the sickening of some of his companions their symptoms so strongly recalled to his mind his own state when sickening with the cow-pox that he very pertinently remarked their striking similarity.

CASE XII.—The paupers of the village of Tortworth, in this county, were inoculated by Mr. Henry Jenner, Surgeon, of Berkeley, in the year 1795. Among them, eight patients presented themselves who had at different periods of their lives had the cow-pox. One of them, Hester Walkley, I attended with that disease when she lived in the service of a farmer in the same village in the year 1782; but neither this woman, nor any other of the patients who had gone through the cow-pox, received the variolous infection either from the arm or from mixing in the society of the other patients who were inoculated at the same time. This state of security proved a fortunate circumstance, as many of the poor women were at the same time in a state of pregnancy.

CASE XIII.—One instance has occurred to me of the system being affected from the matter issuing from the heels of horses, and of its remaining afterwards unsusceptible of the variolous contagion; another, where the smallpox appeared obscurely; and a third, in which its complete existence was positively ascertained.

First, Thomas Pearce is the son of a smith and farrier near to this place. He never had the cow-pox; but, in consequence of dressing horses with sore heels at his father's, when a lad, he had sores on his fingers which suppurated, and which occasioned a pretty severe indisposition. Six years afterwards I inserted variolous matter into his arm repeatedly, without being able to produce any thing more than slight inflammation, which appeared very soon after the matter was applied, and afterwards I exposed him to the contagion of the smallpox with as little effect.[9]

CASE XIV.—Secondly, Mr. James Cole, a farmer in this parish, had a disease from the same source as related in the preceding case, and some years after was inoculated with variolous matter. He had a little pain in the axilla and felt a slight indisposition for three or four hours. A few eruptions shewed themselves on the forehead, but they very soon disappeared without advancing to maturation.

CASE XV.—Although in the former instances the system seemed to be secured, or nearly so, from variolous infection, by the absorption of matter from the sores produced by the diseased heels of horses, yet the following case decisively proves that this cannot be entirely relied upon until a disease has been generated by the morbid matter from the horse on the nipple of the cow, and passed through that medium to the human subject.

Mr. Abraham Riddiford, a farmer at Stone in this parish, in consequence of dressing a mare that had sore heels, was affected with very painful sores in both his hands, tumours in each axilla, and severe and general indisposition. A surgeon in the neighbourhood attended him, who knowing the similarity between the appearance of the sores upon his hands and those produced by the cow-pox, and being acquainted also with the effects of that disease on the human constitution, assured him that he never need to fear the infection of the smallpox; but this assertion proved fallacious,

[9] It is a remarkable fact, and well known to many, that we are frequently foiled in our endeavours to communicate the smallpox by inoculation to blacksmiths, who in the country are farriers. They often, as in the above instance, either resist the contagion entirely, or have the disease anomalously. Shall we not be able to account for this on a rational principle?

for, on being exposed to the infection upwards of twenty years afterwards, he caught the disease, which took its regular course in a very mild way. There certainly was a difference perceptible, although it is not easy to describe it, in the general appearance of the pustules from that which we commonly see. Other practitioners who visited the patient at my request agreed with me in this point, though there was no room left for suspicion as to the reality of the disease, as I inoculated some of his family from the pustules, who had the smallpox, with its usual appearances, in consequence.

Case XVI.—Sarah Nelmes, a dairymaid at a farmer's near this place, was infected with the cow-pox from her master's cows in May, 1796. She received the infection on a part of her hand which had been previously in a slight degree injured by a scratch from a thorn. A large pustulous sore and the usual symptoms accompanying the disease were produced in consequence. The pustule was so expressive of the true character of the cow-pox, as it commonly appears upon the hand, that I have given a representation of it in the annexed plate. The two small pustules on the wrists arose also from the application of the virus to some minute abrasions of the cuticle, but the livid tint, if they ever had any, was not conspicuous at the time I saw the patient. The pustule on the forefinger shews the disease in an earlier stage. It did not actually appear on the hand of this young woman, but was taken from that of another, and is annexed for the purpose of representing the malady after it has newly appeared.

Case XVII.—The more accurately to observe the progress of the infection I selected a healthy boy, about eight years old, for the purpose of inoculation for the cow-pox. The matter was taken from a sore on the hand of a dairymaid,[19] who was infected by her master's cows, and it was inserted, on the 14th of May, 1796, into the arm of the boy by means of two superficial incisions, barely penetrating the cutis, each about half an inch long.

[19] From the sore on the hand of Sarah Nelmes. See the preceding case.

On the seventh day he complained of uneasiness in the axilla, and on the ninth he became a little chilly, lost his appetite, and had a slight headache. During the whole of this day he was perceptibly indisposed, and spent the night with some degree of restlessness, but on the day following he was perfectly well.

The appearance of the incisions in their progress to a state of maturation were much the same as when produced in a similar manner by variolous matter. The only difference which I perceived was in the state of the limpid fluid arising from the action of the virus, which assumed rather a darker hue, and in that of the efflorescence spreading round the incisions, which had more of an erysipelatous look than we commonly perceive when variolous matter has been made use of in the same manner; but the whole died away (leaving on the inoculated parts scabs and subsequent eschars) without giving me or my patient the least trouble.

In order to ascertain whether the boy, after feeling so slight an affection of the system from the cow-pox virus, was secure from the contagion of the smallpox, he was inoculated the 1st of July following with variolous matter, immediately taken from a pustule. Several slight punctures and incisions were made on both his arms, and the matter was carefully inserted, but no disease followed. The same appearances were observable on the arms as we commonly see when a patient has had variolous matter applied, after having either the cow-pox or smallpox. Several months afterwards he was again inoculated with variolous matter, but no sensible effect was produced on the constitution.

Here my researches were interrupted till the spring of the year 1798, when, from the wetness of the early part of the season, many of the farmers' horses in this neighbourhood were affected with sore heels, in consequence of which the cow-pox broke out among several of our dairies, which afforded me an opportunity of making further observations upon this curious disease.

A mare, the property of a person who keeps a dairy in a neighbouring parish, began to have sore heels the latter end of the month of February, 1798, which were occasionally washed by the servant men of the farm, Thomas Virgoe,

William Wherret, and William Haynes, who in consequence became affected with sores in their hands, followed by inflamed lymphatic glands in the arms and axillæ, shiverings succeeded by heat, lassitude, and general pains in the limbs. A single paroxysm terminated the disease; for within twenty-four hours they were free from general indisposition, nothing remaining but the sores on their hands. Haynes and Virgoe, who had gone through the smallpox from inoculation, described their feelings as very similar to those which affected them on sickening with that malady. Wherret never had had the smallpox. Haynes was daily employed as one of the milkers at the farm, and the disease began to shew itself among the cows about ten days after he first assisted in washing the mare's heels. Their nipples became sore in the usual way, with bluish pustules; but as remedies were early applied, they did not ulcerate to any extent.

Case XVIII.—John Baker, a child of five years old, was inoculated March 16, 1798, with matter taken from a pustule on the hand of Thomas Virgoe, one of the servants who had been infected from the mare's heels. He became ill on the sixth day with symptoms similar to those excited by cowpox matter. On the eighth day he was free from indisposition.

There was some variation in the appearance of the pustule on the arm. Although it somewhat resembled a smallpox pustule, yet its similitude was not so conspicuous as when excited by matter from the nipple of the cow, or when the matter has passed from thence through the medium of the human subject.

This experiment was made to ascertain the progress and subsequent effects of the disease when thus propagated. We have seen that the virus from the horse, when it proves infectious to the human subject, is not to be relied upon as rendering the system secure from variolous infection, but that the matter produced by it upon the nipple of the cow is perfectly so. Whether its passing from the horse through the human constitution, as in the present instance, will produce a similar effect, remains to be decided. This would now have been effected, but the boy was rendered unfit for inoculation from having felt the effects of a contagious fever in a workhouse soon after this experiment was made.

CASE XIX.—William Summers, a child of five years and a half old, was inoculated the same day with Baker, with matter taken from the nipples of one of the infected cows, at the farm alluded to. He became indisposed on the sixth day, vomited once, and felt the usual slight symptoms till the eighth day, when he appeared perfectly well. The progress of the pustule, formed by the infection of the virus, was similar to that noticed in Case XVII, with this exception, its being free from the livid tint observed in that instance.

CASE XX.—From William Summers the disease was transferred to William Pead, a boy of eight years old, who was inoculated March 28th. On the sixth day he complained of pain in the axilla, and on the seventh was affected with the common symptoms of a patient sickening with the smallpox from inoculation, which did not terminate till the third day after the seizure. So perfect was the similarity to the variolous fever that I was induced to examine the skin, conceiving there might have been some eruptions, but none appeared. The efflorescent blush around the part punctured in the boy's arm was so truly characteristic of that which appears on variolous inoculation that I have given a representation of it. The drawing was made when the pustule was beginning to die away and the areola retiring from the centre.

CASE XXI.—April 5th: Several children and adults were inoculated from the arm of William Pead. The greater part of them sickened on the sixth day, and were well on the seventh, but in three of the number a secondary indisposition arose in consequence of an extensive erysipelatous inflammation which appeared on the inoculated arms. It seemed to arise from the state of the pustule, which spread out, accompanied with some degree of pain, to about half the diameter of a sixpence. One of these patients was an infant of half a year old. By the application of mercurial ointment to the inflamed parts (a treatment recommended under similar circumstances in the inoculated smallpox) the complaint subsided without giving much trouble.

Hannah Excell, an healthy girl of seven years old, and one of the patients above mentioned, received the infection from the insertion of the virus under the cuticle of the arm in three distinct points. The pustules which arose in consequence so much resembled, on the twelfth day, those appearing from the infection of variolous matter, that an experienced inoculator would scarcely have discovered a shade of difference at that period. Experience now tells me that almost the only variation which follows consists in the pustulous fluids remaining limpid nearly to the time of its total disappearance; and not, as in the direct smallpox, becoming purulent.

CASE XXII.—From the arm of this girl matter was taken and inserted April 12th into the arms of John Macklove, one year and a half old, Robert F. Jenner, eleven months old, Mary Pead, five years old, and Mary James, six years old.

Among these, Robert F. Jenner did not receive the infection. The arms of the other three inflamed properly and began to affect the system in the usual manner; but being under some apprehensions from the preceding cases that a troublesome erysipelas might arise, I determined on making an experiment with the view of cutting off its source. Accordingly, after the patients had felt an indisposition of about twelve hours, I applied in two of these cases out of the three, on the vesicle formed by the virus, a little mild caustic, composed of equal parts of quick-lime and soap, and suffered it to remain on the part six hours.[11] It seemed to give the children but little uneasiness, and effectually answered my intention in preventing the appearance of erysipelas. Indeed, it seemed to do more, for in half an hour after its application the indisposition of the children ceased.[12] These precautions were perhaps unnecessary, as the arm of the third child, Mary Pead, which was suffered to take its common course, scabbed quickly, without any erysipelas.

[11] Perhaps a few touches with the lapis septicus would have proved equally efficacious.
[12] What effect would a similar treatment produce in inoculation for the smallpox?

CASE XXIII.—From this child's arm matter was taken and transferred to that of J. Barge, a boy of seven years old. He sickened on the eighth day, went through the disease with the usual slight symptoms, and without any inflammation on the arm beyond the common efflorescence surrounding the pustule, an appearance so often seen in inoculated smallpox.

After the many fruitless attempts to give the smallpox to those who had had the cow-pox, it did not appear necessary, nor was it convenient to me, to inoculate the whole of those who had been the subjects of these late trials; yet I thought it right to see the effects of variolous matter on some of them, particularly William Summers, the first of these patients who had been infected with matter taken from the cow. He was, therefore, inoculated with variolous matter from a fresh pustule; but, as in the preceding cases, the system did not feel the effects of it in the smallest degree. I had an opportunity also of having this boy and William Pead inoculated by my nephew, Mr. Henry Jenner, whose report to me is as follows: " I have inoculated Pead and Barge, two of the boys whom you lately infected with the cow-pox. On the second day the incisions were inflamed and there was a pale inflammatory stain around them. On the third day these appearances were still increasing and their arms itched considerably. On the fourth day the inflammation was evidently subsiding, and on the sixth day it was scarcely perceptible. No symptom of indisposition followed.

"To convince myself that the variolous matter made use of was in a perfect state I at the same time inoculated a patient with some of it who never had gone through the cow-pox, and it produced the smallpox in the usual regular manner."

These experiments afforded me much satisfaction; they proved that the matter, in passing from one human subject to another, through five gradations, lost none of its original properties, J. Barge being the fifth who received the infection successively from William Summers, the boy to whom it was communicated from the cow.

I shall now conclude this inquiry with some general observations on the subject, and on some others which are interwoven with it.

Although I presume it may be unnecessary to produce further testimony in support of my assertion "that the cow-pox protects the human constitution from the infection of the smallpox," yet it affords me considerable satisfaction to say that Lord Somerville, the President of the Board of Agriculture, to whom this paper was shewn by Sir Joseph Banks, has found upon inquiry that the statements were confirmed by the concurring testimony of Mr. Dolland, a surgeon, who resides in a dairy country remote from this, in which these observations were made. With respect to the opinion adduced " that the source of the infection is a peculiar morbid matter arising in the horse," although I have not been able to prove it from actual experiments conducted immediately under my own eye, yet the evidence I have adduced appears sufficient to establish it.

They who are not in the habit of conducting experiments may not be aware of the coincidence of circumstances necessary for their being managed so as to prove perfectly decisive; nor how often men engaged in professional pursuits are liable to interruptions which disappoint them almost at the instant of their being accomplished: however, I feel no room for hesitation respecting the common origin of the disease, being well convinced that it never appears among the cows (except it can be traced to a cow introduced among the general herd which has been previously infected, or to an infected servant) unless they have been milked by some one who, at the same time, has the care of a horse affected with diseased heels.

The spring of the year 1797, which I intended particularly to have devoted to the completion of this investigation, proved, from its dryness, remarkably adverse to my wishes; for it frequently happens, while the farmers' horses are exposed to the cold rains which fall at that season, that their heels become diseased, and no cow-pox then appeared in the neighbourhood.

The active quality of the virus from the horses' heels is **greatly increased after it has acted on the nipples of the** cow, as it rarely happens that the horse affects his dresser with sores, and as rarely that a milkmaid escapes the infection when she milks infected cows. It is most active at the commencement of the disease, even before it has acquired a pus-like appearance; indeed, I am not confident whether this property in the matter does not entirely cease as soon as it is secreted in the form of pus. I am induced to think it does cease,[13] and that it is the thin, darkish-looking fluid only, oozing from the newly-formed cracks in the heels, similar to what sometimes appears from erysipelatous blisters, which gives the disease. Nor am I certain that the nipples of the cows are at all times in a state to receive the infection. The appearance of the disease in the spring and the early part of the summer, when they are disposed to be affected with spontaneous eruptions so much more frequently than at other seasons, induces me to think that the virus from the horse must be received upon them when they are in this state, in order to produce effects: experiments, however, must determine these points. But it is clear that when the cow-pox virus is once generated, that the cows cannot resist the contagion, in whatever state their nipples may chance to be, if they are milked with an infected hand.

Whether the matter, either from the cow or the horse, will affect the sound skin of the human body, I cannot positively determine; probably it will not, unless on those parts where the cuticle is extremely thin, as on the lips, for example. I have known an instance of a poor girl who produced an ulceration on her lip by frequently holding her finger to her mouth to cool the raging of a cow-pox sore by blowing upon it. The hands of the farmers' servants here, from the nature of their employments, are constantly exposed to those injuries which occasion abrasions of the cuticle, to punctures from thorns, and such like accidents; so that they are always in a state to feel the consequence of exposure to infectious matter.

It is singular to observe that the cow-pox virus, although

[13] It is very easy to procure pus from old sores on the heels of horses. This I have often inserted into scratches made with a lancet, on the sound nipples of cows, and have seen no other effects from it than simple inflammation.

it renders the constitution unsusceptible of the variolous, should nevertheless, leave it unchanged with respect to its own action. I have already produced an instance [14] to point out this, and shall now corroborate it with another.

Elizabeth Wynne, who had the cow-pox in the year 1759, was inoculated with variolous matter, without effect, in the year 1797, and again caught the cow-pox in the year 1798. When I saw her, which was on the eighth day after she received the infection, I found her affected with general lassitude, shiverings, alternating with heat, coldness of the extremities, and a quick and irregular pulse. These symptoms were preceded by a pain in the axilla. On her hand was one large pustulous sore, which resembled that delineated in Plate No. 1. (Plate appears in original.)

It is curious also to observe that the virus, which with respect to its effects is undetermined and uncertain previously to its passing from the horse through the medium of the cow, should then not only become more active, but should invariably and completely possess those specific properties which induce in the human constitution symptoms similar to those of the variolous fever, and effect in it that peculiar change which for ever renders it unsusceptible of the variolous contagion.

May it not then be reasonably conjectured that the source of the smallpox is morbid matter of a peculiar kind, generated by a disease in the horse, and that accidental circumstances may have again and again arisen, still working new changes upon it until it has acquired the contagious and malignant form under which we now commonly see it making its devastations amongst us? And, from a consideration of the change which the infectious matter undergoes from producing a disease on the cow, may we not conceive that many contagious diseases, now prevalent among us, may owe their present appearance not to a simple, but to a compound, origin? For example, is it difficult to imagine that the measles, the scarlet fever, and the ulcerous sore throat with a spotted skin have all sprung from the same source, assuming some variety in their forms according to the nature of their new

[14] See Case IX.

combinations? The same question will apply respecting the origin of many other contagious diseases which bear a strong analogy to each other.

There are certainly more forms than one, without considering the common variation between the confluent and distinct, in which the smallpox appears in what is called the natural way. About seven years ago a species of smallpox spread through many of the towns and villages of this part of Gloucestershire: it was of so mild a nature that a fatal instance was scarcely ever heard of, and consequently so little dreaded by the lower orders of the community that they scrupled not to hold the same intercourse with each other as if no infectious disease had been present among them. I never saw nor heard of an instance of its being confluent. The most accurate manner, perhaps, in which I can convey an idea of it is by saying that had fifty individuals been taken promiscuously and infected by exposure to this contagion, they would have had as mild and light a disease as if they had been inoculated with variolous matter in the usual way. The harmless manner in which it shewed itself could not arise from any peculiarity either in the season or the weather, for I watched its progress upwards of a year without perceiving any variation in its general appearance. I consider it then as a *variety* of the smallpox.[15]

In some of the preceding cases I have noticed the attention that was paid to the state of the variolous matter previous to the experiment of inserting it into the arms of those who had gone through the cow-pox. This I conceived to be of great importance in conducting these experiments, and, were it always properly attended to by those who inoculate for the smallpox, it might prevent much subsequent mischief and confusion. With the view of enforcing so necessary a precaution I shall take the liberty of digressing so far as to point out some unpleasant facts relative to mismanagement in this particular, which have fallen under my own observation.

[15] My friend, Dr. Hicks, of Bristol, who, during the prevalence of this distemper, was resident at Gloucester, and physician of the hospital there (where it was seen soon after its first appearance in this country), had opportunities of making numerous observations upon it, which it is his intention to communicate to the public.

A medical gentleman (now no more), who for many years inoculated in this neighbourhood, frequently preserved the variolous matter intended for his use on a piece of lint or cotton, which, in its fluid state, was put into a vial, corked, and conveyed into a warm pocket; a situation certainly favourable for speedily producing putrefaction in it. In this state (not unfrequently after it had been taken several days from the pustules) it was inserted into the arms of his patients, and brought on inflammation of the incised parts, swellings of the axillary glands, fever, and sometimes eruptions. But what was this disease? Certainly not the smallpox; for the matter having from putrefaction lost or suffered a derangement in its specific properties, was no longer capable of producing that malady, those who had been inoculated in this manner being as much subject to the contagion of the smallpox as if they had never been under the influence of this artificial disease; and many, unfortunately, fell victims to it, who thought themselves in perfect security. The same unfortunate circumstance of giving a disease, supposed to be the smallpox, with inefficacious variolous matter, having occurred under the direction of some other practitioners within my knowledge, and probably from the same incautious method of securing the variolous matter, I avail myself of this opportunity of mentioning what I conceive to be of great importance; and, as a further cautionary hint, I shall again digress so far as to add another observation on the subject of inoculation.

Whether it be yet ascertained by experiment that the quantity of variolous matter inserted into the skin makes any difference with respect to the subsequent mildness or violence of the disease, I know not; but I have the strongest reason for supposing that if either the punctures or incisions be made so deep as to go *through* it and wound the adipose membrane, that the risk of bringing on a violent disease is greatly increased. I have known an inoculator whose practice was "to cut deep enough (to use his own expression) to see a bit of fat." and there to lodge the matter. The great number of bad cases, independent of inflammations and abscesses on the arms, and the fatality which attended this practice, was almost inconceivable; and I cannot account for ît on any other principle than that of the matter being placed in this situation instead of the skin.

It was the practice of another, whom I well remember, to pinch up a small portion of the skin on the arms of his patients and to pass through it a needle, with a thread attached to it previously dipped in variolous matter. The thread was lodged in the perforated part, and consequently left in contact with the cellular membrane. This practice was attended with the same ill success as the former. Although it is very improbable that any one would now inoculate in this rude way by design, yet these observations may tend to place a double guard over the lancet, when infants, whose skins are comparatively so very thin, fall under the care of the inoculator.

A very respectable friend of mine, Dr. Hardwicke, of Sodbury, in this county, inoculated great numbers of patients previous to the introduction of the more modern method by Sutton, and with such success that a fatal instance occurred as rarely as since that method has been adopted. It was the doctor's practice to make as slight an incision as possible *upon* the skin, and there to lodge a thread saturated with the variolous matter. When his patients became indisposed, agreeably to the custom then prevailing, they were directed to go to bed and were kept moderately warm. Is it not probable then that the success of the modern practice may depend more upon the method of invariably depositing the virus in or upon the skin, than on the subsequent treatment of the disease?

I do not mean to insinuate that exposure to cool air, and suffering the patient to drink cold water when hot and thirsty, may not moderate the eruptive symptoms and lessen the number of pustules; yet, to repeat my former observation, I cannot account for the uninterrupted success, or nearly so, of one practitioner, and the wretched state of the patients under the care of another, where, in both instances, the general treatment did not differ essentially, without conceiving it to arise from the different modes of inserting the matter for the purpose of producing the disease. As it is not the identical matter inserted which is absorbed into the constitution, but that which is, by some peculiar process in the animal

economy, generated by it, is it not probable that differen.
parts of the human body may prepare or modify the virus
differently? Although the skin, for example, adipose membrane, or mucous membranes are all capable of producing
the variolous virus by the stimulus given by the particles
originally deposited upon them, yet I am induced to conceive
that each of these parts is capable of producing some variation in the qualities of the matter previous to its affecting
the constitution. What else can constitute the difference between the smallpox when communicated casually or in what
has been termed the natural way, or when brought on artificially through the medium of the skin?

After all, are the variolous particles, possessing their true
specific and contagious principles, ever taken up and conveyed by the lymphatics unchanged into the blood vessels? I
imagine not. Were this the case, should we not find the blood
sufficiently loaded with them in some stages of the smallpox
to communicate the disease by inserting it under the cuticle,
or by spreading it on the surface of an ulcer? Yet experiments have determined the impracticability of its being given
in this way; although it has been proved that variolous
matter, when much diluted with water and applied to the
skin in the usual manner, will produce the disease. But it
would be digressing beyond a proper boundary to go minutely
into this subject here.

At what period the cow-pox was first noticed here is not
upon record. Our oldest farmers were not unacquainted with
it in their earliest days, when it appeared among their farms
without any deviation from the phænomena which it now ex-
hibits. Its connection with the smallpox seems to have been
unknown to them. Probably the general introduction of
inoculation first occasioned the discovery.

Its rise in this country may not have been of very remote
date, as the practice of milking cows might formerly have
been in the hands of women only; which I believe is the case
now in some other dairy countries, and, consequently, that
the cows might not in former times have been exposed to the
contagious matter brought by the men servants from the
heels of horses.[16] Indeed, a knowledge of the source of the

[16] I have been informed from respectable authority that in Ireland, al-

infection is new in the minds of most of the farmers in this neighbourhood, but it has at length produced good consequences; and it seems probable, from the precautions they are now disposed to adopt, that the appearance of the cowpox here may either be entirely extinguished or become extremely rare.

Should it be asked whether this investigation is a matter of mere curiosity, or whether it tends to any beneficial purpose, I should answer that, notwithstanding the happy effects of inoculation, with all the improvements which the practice has received since its first introduction into this country, it not very unfrequently produces deformity of the skin, and sometimes, under the best management, proves fatal.

These circumstances must naturally create in every instance some degree of painful solicitude for its consequences. But as I have never known fatal effects arise from the cowpox, even when impressed in the most unfavourable manner, producing extensive inflammations and suppurations on the hands; and as it clearly appears that this disease leaves the constitution in a state of perfect security from the infection of the smallpox, may we not infer that a mode of inoculation may be introduced preferable to that at present adopted, especially among those families which, from previous circumstances, we may judge to be predisposed to have the disease unfavourably? It is an excess in the number of pustules which we chiefly dread in the smallpox; but in the cow-pox no pustules appear, nor does it seem possible for the contagious matter to produce the disease from effluvia, or by any other means than contact, and that probably not simply between the virus and the cuticle; so that a single individual in a family might at any time receive it without the risk of infecting the rest or of spreading a distemper that fills a country with terror.

Several instances have come under my observation which justify the assertion that the disease cannot be propagated by effluvia. The first boy whom I inoculated with the matter

though dairies abound in many parts of the island, the disease is entirely unknown. The reason seems obvious. The business of the dairy is conducted by women only. Were the meanest vassal among the men employed there as a milker at a dairy, he would feel his situation unpleasant beyond all endurance.

of cow-pox slept in a bed, while the experiment was going forward, with two children who never had gone through either that disease or the smallpox, without infecting either of them.

A young woman who had the cow-pox to a great extent, several sores which maturated having appeared on the hands and wrists, slept in the same bed with a fellow-dairymaid who never had been infected with either the cow-pox or the smallpox, but no indisposition followed.

Another instance has occurred of a young woman on whose hands were several large suppurations from the cow-pox, who was at the same time a daily nurse to an infant, but the complaint was not communicated to the child.

In some other points of view the inoculation of this disease appears preferable to the variolous inoculation.

In constitutions predisposed to scrophula, how frequently we see the inoculated smallpox rouse into activity that distressful malady! This circumstance does not seem to depend on the manner in which the distemper has shewn itself, for it has as frequently happened among those who have had it mildly as when it has appeared in the contrary way.

There are many who, from some peculiarity in the habit, resist the common effects of variolous matter inserted into the skin, and who are in consequence haunted through life with the distressing idea of being insecure from subsequent infection. A ready mode of dissipating anxiety originating from such a cause must now appear obvious. And, as we have seen that the constitution may at any time be made to feel the febrile attack of cow-pox, might it not, in many chronic diseases, be introduced into the system, with the probability of affording relief, upon well-known physiological principles?

Although I say the system may at any time be made to feel the febrile attack of cow-pox, yet I have a single instance before me where the virus acted locally only, but it is not in the least probable that the same person would resist the action both of the cow-pox virus and the variolous.

Elizabeth Sarfenet lived as a dairymaid at Newpark farm, in this parish. All the cows and the servants employed in milking had the cow-pox; but this woman, though she had several sores upon her fingers, felt no tumours in the axillæ, nor any general indisposition. On being afterwards casually exposed to variolous infection, she had the smallpox in a mild way. Hannah Pick, another of the dairymaids who was a fellow-servant with Elizabeth Sarfenet when the distemper broke out at the farm, was, at the same time, infected; but this young woman had not only sores upon her hands, but felt herself also much indisposed for a day or two. After this, I made several attempts to give her the smallpox by inoculation, but they all proved fruitless. From the former case then we see that the animal economy is subject to the same laws in one disease as the other.

The following case, which has very lately occurred, renders it highly probable that not only the heels of the horse, but other parts of the body of that animal, are capable of generating the virus which produces the cow-pox.

An extensive inflammation of the erysipelatous kind appeared without any apparent cause upon the upper part of the thigh of a sucking colt, the property of Mr. Millet, a farmer at Rockhampton, a village near Berkeley. The inflammation continued several weeks, and at length terminated in the formation of three or four small abscesses. The inflamed parts were fomented, and dressings were applied by some of the same persons who were employed in milking the cows. The number of cows milked was twenty-four, and the whole of them had the cow-pox. The milkers, consisting of the farmer's wife, a man and a maidservant, were infected by the cows. The man-servant had previously gone through the smallpox, and felt but little of the cow-pox. The servant maid had some years before been infected with the cow-pox, and she also felt it now in a slight degree; but the farmer's wife, who never had gone through either of the diseases, felt its effects very severely.

That the disease produced upon the cows by the colt and from thence conveyed to those who milked them was the *true* and not the *spurious* cow-pox, there can be scarcely any room for suspicion; yet it would have been more completely satisfactory had the effects of variolous matter been ascertained on the farmer's wife, but there was a peculiarity in her situation which prevented my making the experiment.

Thus far have I proceeded in an inquiry founded, as it must appear, on the basis of experiment; in which, however, conjecture has been occasionally admitted in order to present to persons well situated for such discussions objects for a more minute investigation. In the mean time I shall myself continue to prosecute this inquiry, encouraged by the hope of its becoming essentially beneficial to mankind.

II

FURTHER OBSERVATIONS ON THE VARIOLÆ VACCINÆ, OR COW-POX. 1799

ALTHOUGH it has not been in my power to extend the inquiry into the causes and effects of the variolæ vaccinæ much beyond its original limits, yet, perceiving that it is beginning to excite a general spirit of investigation, I think it of importance, without delay, to communicate such facts as have since occurred, and to point out. the fallacious sources from whence a disease imitative of the true variolæ vaccinæ might arise, with the view of preventing those who may inoculate from producing a spurious disease; and, further, to enforce the precaution suggested in the former treatise on the subject, of subduing the inoculated pustule as soon as it has sufficiently produced its influence on the constitution. From a want of due discrimination of the real existence of the disease, either in the brute or in the human subject, and also of that stage of it in which it is capable of producing the change in the animal economy which renders it unsusceptible of the contagion of the smallpox, unpleasant consequences might ensue, the source of which, perhaps, might not be suspected by one inexperienced in conducting such experiments.

My late publication contains a relation of most of the facts which had come under my own inspection at the time it was written, interspersed with some conjectural observations. Since then Dr. G. Pearson has established an inquiry into the validity of my principal assertion, the result of which cannot but be highly flattering to my feelings. It contains not a single case which I think can be called an exception to the fact I was so firmly impressed with—that the cow-pox protects the human body from the smallpox. I have myself received some further confirmations, which shall be subjoined. I have lately also been favoured with a letter from a gentleman of great respectability (Dr. Ingenhousz), informing me that, on making an inquiry into the subject in the county of Wilts, he discovered that a farmer near Calne had been infected with the smallpox after having had the cow-pox, and that the disease in each instance was so strongly characterized as to render the facts incontrovertible. The cow-pox, it seems, from the doctor's information, was communicated to the farmer from his cows at the time that they gave out *an offensive stench from their udders.*

Some other instances have likewise been represented to me of the appearance of the disease, apparently marked with its characteristic symptoms, and yet that the patients have afterwards had the smallpox. On these cases I shall, for the present, suspend any particular remarks, but hope that the general observations I have to offer in the sequel will prove of sufficient weight to render the idea of their ever having had existence, but as cases of spurious cow-pox, extremely doubtful.

Ere I proceed let me be permitted to observe that truth, in this and every other physiological inquiry that has occupied my attention, has ever been the object of my pursuit, and should it appear in the present instance that I have been led into error, fond as I may appear of the offspring of my labours, I had rather see it perish at once than exist and do a public injury.

I shall proceed to enumerate the sources, or what appear to me as such, of a spurious cow-pox.

First: That arising from pustules on the nipples or udder of the cow; which pustules contain no specific virus.

Secondly: From matter (although originally possessing the specific virus) which has suffered a decomposition, either from putrefaction or from any other cause less obvious to the senses.

Thirdly: From matter taken from an ulcer in an advanced stage, which ulcer arose from a true cow pock.

Fourthly: From matter produced on the human skin from contact with some peculiar morbid matter generated by a horse.

On these subjects I shall offer some comments: First, to what length pustulous diseases of the udder and nipples of the cow may extend it is not in my power to determine; but certain it is that these parts of the animal are subject to some variety of maladies of this nature; and as many of these eruptions (probably all of them) are capable of giving a disease to the human body, would it not be discreet for those engaged in this investigation to suspend controversy and cavil until they can ascertain with precision what *is* and what *is not* the cow-pox?

For example: A farmer who is not conversant with any of these maladies, but who may have heard of the cow-pox in general terms, may acquaint a neighbouring surgeon that the distemper appears at his farm. The surgeon, eager to make an experiment, takes away matter, inoculates, produces a sore, uneasiness in the axilla, and perhaps some affection of the system. This is one way in which a fallacious idea of security both in the mind of the inoculator and the patient may arise; for a disease may thus have been propagated from a simple eruption only.

One of the first objects then of this pursuit, as I have observed, should be, to learn how to distinguish with accuracy between that peculiar pustule which is the *true* cow pock, and that which is spurious. Until experience has determined this, we view our object through a mist. Let us, for instance, suppose that the smallpox and the chicken-pox were at the same time to spread among the inhabitants of a country which had never been visited by either of these distempers, and where they were quite unknown before: what confusion would arise! The resemblance between the symptoms of the eruptive fever and between the pustules in either case would be so striking that a patient who had gone through the chicken-pox to any extent would feel equally easy with regard to his future security from the smallpox as the person who had actually passed through that disease. Time and future observation would draw the line of distinction.

So I presume it will be with the cow-pox until it is more

generally understood. All cavilling, therefore, on the mere report of those who *tell us* they have had this distemper, and are afterwards found susceptible of the smallpox, should be suspended. To illustrate this I beg leave to give the following history:

Sarah Merlin, of the parish of Eastington in this county, when about thirteen or fourteen years of age lived as a servant with farmer Clarke, who kept a dairy consisting of about eighteen cows at Stonehouse, a neighbouring village. The nipples and udders of three of the cows were extensively affected with large white blisters. These cows the girl milked daily, and at the time she assisted, with two others, in milking the rest of the herd. It soon appeared that the disease was communicated to the girl. The rest of the cows escaped the infection, although they were milked several days after the three above specified, had these eruptions on the nipples and udders, and even after the girl's hand became sore. The two others who were engaged in milking, although they milked the cows indiscriminately, received no injury. On the fingers of each of the girl's hands there appeared several large white blisters—she supposes about three or four on each finger. The hands and arms inflamed and swelled, but no constitutional indisposition followed. The sores were anointed with some domestic ointment and got well without ulcerating.

As this malady was called the cow-pox, and recorded as such in the mind of the patient, she became regardless of the smallpox; but, on being exposed to it some years afterwards she was infected, and had a full burthen.

Now had any one conversant with the habits of the disease heard this history, they would have had no hesitation in pronouncing it a case of spurious cow-pox; considering its deviation in the *numerous* blisters which appeared on the girl's hands; their termination without ulceration; its not proving more generally contagious at the farm, either among the cattle or those employed in milking; and considering also that *the patient felt no general indisposition, although there was so great a number of vesicles.*

This is perhaps the most deceptious form in which an eruptive disease can be communicated from the cow, and it

certainly requires some attention in discriminating it. The
most perfect criterion by which the judgment may be guided
is perhaps that adopted by those who attend infected cattle.
These white blisters on the nipples, they say, *never eat into
the fleshy parts* like those which are commonly of a bluish
cast, and which constitute the *true cow-pox*, but that they
affect the skin only, quickly end in scabs, and are not nearly
so infectious.

That which appeared to me as one cause of spurious eruptions, I have already remarked in the former treatise, namely, the transition that the cow makes in the spring from a
poor to a nutritious diet, and from the udder's becoming at
this time more vascular than usual for the supply of milk.
But there is another source of inflammation and pustules
which I believe is not uncommon in all the dairy counties in
the west of England. A cow intended to be exposed for sale,
having naturally a small udder, is previously for a day or
two neither milked artificially nor is her calf suffered to have
access to her. Thus the milk is preternaturally accumulated,
and the udder and nipples become greatly distended. The
consequences frequently are inflammation and eruptions
which maturate.

Whether a disease generated in this way has the power of
affecting the constitution in any *peculiar* manner I cannot
presume positively to determine. It has been conjectured to
have been a cause of the true cow-pox, though my inquiries
have not led me to adopt this supposition in any one instance; on the contrary, I have known the milkers affected
by it, but always found that an affection thus induced left the
system as susceptible of the smallpox as before.

What is advanced in my second position I consider also of
very great importance, and I could wish it to be strongly impressed on the minds of all who may be disposed to conclude
hastily on my observations, whether engaged in their investigation by experiments or not. To place this in its clearest
point of view (as the similarity between the action of the
smallpox and the cow-pox matter is so obvious) it will be
necessary to consider what we sometimes observe to take
place in inoculation for the smallpox when imperfect variolous matter is made use of. The concise history on this sub-

ject that was brought forward respecting what I had observed in this neighbourhood[1] I perceive, by a reference since made to the Memoirs of the Medical Society of London, may be considered as no more than a corroboration of the facts very clearly detailed by Mr. Kite.[2] To this copious evidence I have to add still more in the following communications from Mr. Earle, surgeon, of Frampton-upon-Severn, in this county, which I deem the more valuable, as he has with much candour permitted me to make them public:

" SIR:

" I have read with satisfaction your late publication on the Variolæ Vaccinæ, and being, among many other curious circumstances, particularly struck with that relating to the inefficacy of smallpox matter in a particular state, I think it proper to lay before you the following facts which came within my own knowledge, and which certainly tend to strengthen the opinions advanced in pages 56 and 57 of your treatise.

" In March, 1784, a general inoculation took place at Arlingham in this county. I inoculated several patients with active variolous matter, all of whom had the disease in a favourable way; but the matter being all used, and not being able to procure any more in the state I wished, I was under the necessity of taking it from a pustule which, experience has since proved, was advanced too far to answer the purpose I intended. Of five persons inoculated with this last matter, four took the smallpox afterwards in the natural way, one of whom died, three recovered, and the other, being cautioned by me to avoid as much as possible the chance of catching it, escaped from the disease through life. He died of another disorder about two years ago.

" Although one of these cases ended unfortunate, yet I cannot suppose that any medical man will think me careless or inattentive in their management; for I conceive the appearances were such as might have induced any one to sup-

---

[1] Inquiry into the Causes and Effects of the Variolæ Vaccinæ, p. 56 of the original article.
[2] See an account of some anomalous appearances consequent to the inoculation of the smallpox, by Charles Kite, Surgeon, of Gravesend, in the Memoirs of the Medical Society of London, vol. iv. p. 114.

pose that the persons were perfectly safe from future infection. Inflammation in every case took place in the arm, and fever came on with a considerable degree of pain in the axilla. In some of their arms the inflammation and suppuration were more violent than is commonly observed when perfect matter is made use of; in one there was an ulcer which cast off several large sloughs. About the ninth day eruptions appeared, which died away earlier than common without maturation. From these circumstances I should suppose that no medical practitioner would scarcely have entertained a doubt but that these patients had been infected with a true smallpox; yet I must confess that some small degree of doubt presented itself to me at the speedy disappearance of the eruptions; and in order, as far as I could, to ascertain their safety, I sent one of them to a much older practitioner than myself. This gentleman, on hearing the circumstances of the case, pronounced the patient perfectly secure from future infection.

"The following facts are also a striking proof of the truth of your observations on this subject:

"In the year 1789 I inoculated three children of Mr. Coaley, of Hurst farm in this county. The arms inflamed properly, fever and pain in the axillæ came on precisely the same as in the former cases, and in ten days eruptions appeared, which disappeared in the course of two days. I must observe that the matter here made use of was procured for me by a friend; but no doubt it was in an improper state; for, from the similarity of these cases to those which happened at Arlingham five years before, I was somewhat alarmed for their safety, and desired to inoculate them again: which being permitted, I was particularly careful to procure matter in its most perfect state. All the children took the smallpox from this second inoculation, and all had a very full burthen. These facts I conceive strikingly corroborate your opinion relative to the different states of matter; for in both instances that I have mentioned it was capable of producing something strongly resembling the true smallpox, although it afterwards proved not to be so.

"As I think the communication of these cases is a duty

I owe to the public, you are at liberty to make what use you please of this letter.   I remain, &c.,

"John Earle.

"FRAMPTON-UPON SEVERN, GLOUCESTERSHIRE, November 10, 1798.

"P. S. I think it necessary to observe that I can pronounce, with the greatest certainty, that the matter with which the Arlingham patients were inoculated was taken from a true smallpox pustule. I took it myself from a subject that had a very full burthen."

Certain then it is that variolous matter may undergo such a change from the putrefactive process, as well as from some of the more obscure and latent processes of nature, as will render it incapable of giving the smallpox in such a manner as to secure the human constitution from future infection, although we see at the same time it is capable of exciting a disease which bears so strong a resemblance to it as to produce inflammation and matter in the incised skin (frequently, indeed, more violent than when it produces its effects perfectly), swelling of the axillary glands, general indisposition, and eruptions. So strongly persuaded was the gentleman, whose practice I have mentioned in page 56 of the late treatise, that he could produce a mild smallpox by his mode of managing the matter, that he spoke of it as a useful discovery until convinced of his error by the fatal consequence which ensued.

After this ought we to be in the smallest degree surprised to find, among a great number of individuals who, by living in dairies, have been casually exposed to the cow-pox virus when in a state analogous to that of the smallpox above described, some who may have had the disease so imperfectly as not to render them secure from variolous attacks? For the matter, when burst from the pustules on the nipples of the cow, by being exposed, from its lodgment there, to the heat of an inflamed surface, and from being at the same time in a situation to be occasionally moistened with milk, is often likely to be in a state conducive to putrefaction; and thus, under some modification of decomposition, it must, of course, sometimes find access to the hand of the milker in such a way as to infect him. What confusion should we have were there no other mode of inoculating the smallpox than such as would happen from handling the diseased skin of a person labouring under that distemper in some of its advanced and loathsome stages! It must be observed that every case of cow-pox in the human species, whether communicated by design or otherwise, is to be considered as a case of inoculation. And here I may be allowed to make an observation on the case of the farmer communicated to me by Dr. Ingenhousz. That he was exposed to the matter when it had undergone the putrefactive change is highly probable from the doctor's observing that the sick cows at the farm gave out an *offensive stench from their udders.* However, I must remark that it is unusual for cattle to suffer to such an extent, when disordered with the cow-pox, as to make a bystander sensible of any ill smell. I have often stood among a herd which had the distemper without being conscious of its presence from any particular effluvia. Indeed, in this neighbourhood it commonly receives an early check from escharotic applications of the *cow leech.* It has been conceived to be contagious without contact; but this idea cannot be well founded because the cattle in one meadow do not infect those in another (although there may be no other partition than a hedge) unless they be handled or milked by those who bring the infectious matter with them; and of course, the smallest particle imaginable, when applied to a part susceptible of its influence, may produce the effect. Among the human species it appears to be very clear that the disease is produced by contact only. All my attempts, at least, to communicate it by effluvia have hitherto proved ineffectual.

As well as the perfect change from that state in which variolous matter is capable of producing full and decisive effects on the constitution, to that wherein its specific properties are entirely lost, it may reasonably be supposed that it is capable of undergoing a variety of intermediate changes. The following singular occurrences in ten cases of inoculation, obligingly communicated to me by Mr. Trye, Senior Surgeon to the Infirmary at Glocester, seem to indicate that the variolous matter, previously to its being taken

from the patient for the intended purpose, was beginning
to part with some of its original properties, or, in other
words, that it had suffered a partial decomposition. Mr.
Trye says: " I inoculated ten children with matter taken at
one time and from the same subject. I observed no peculiarity in any of them previously to their inoculation, nor
did any thing remarkable appear in their arms till after
the decline of the disease. Two infants of three months old
had erysipelas about the incisions, in one of them extending
from the shoulders to the fingers' ends. Another infant
had abscesses in the cellular substance in the neighbourhood of the incisions, and five or six of the rest had axillary
abscesses. The matter was taken from the distinct smallpox late in its progress, and when some pustules had been
dried. It was received upon glass and slowly dried by the
fire. All the children had pustules which maturated, so
that I suppose them all secure from future infection; at
least, as secure as any others whom I have ever inoculated.
My practice never afforded a sore arm before."

In regard to my former observation on the improper and
dangerous mode of preserving variolous matter, I shall here
remark that it seems not to have been clearly understood.
Finding that it has been confounded with the more eligible
modes of preservation, I will explain myself further. When
the matter is taken from a fit pustule and properly prepared
for preservation, it may certainly be kept without losing its
specific properties a great length of time; for instance, when ·
it is previously dried in the open air on some compact body,
as a quill or a piece of glass, and afterwards secured in a
small vial.[3] But when kept several days in a state of mois-
ture, and during that time exposed to a warm temperature,
I do not think it can be relied upon as capable of giving a
perfect disease, although, as I have before observed, the
progress of the symptoms arising from the action of the
imperfect matter bear so strong a resemblance to the smallpox when excited completely.

Thirdly. That the first formed virus, or what constitutes
the true cow-pox pustule, invariably possesses the power I

[3] Thus prepared, the cow-pox virus was found perfectly active, and possessing all its specific properties, at the end of three months.

have ascribed to it, namely, that of affecting the constitution with a specific disease, is a truth that no subsequent occurrence has yet led me to doubt. But as I am now endeavouring to guard the public as much as possible against erroneous conclusions, I shall observe that when this pustule has degenerated into an ulcer (to which state it is often disposed to pass unless timely checked), I suspect that matter possessing very different properties may sooner or later be produced; and although it may have passed that stage wherein the specific properties of the matter secreted are no longer present in it, yet when applied to a sore (as in the casual way) it might dispose that sore to ulcerate, and from its irritation the system would probably become affected; and thus, by assuming some of its strongest characters, it would imitate the genuine cow-pox.

From the preceding observations on the matter of small-pox when decomposed it must, I conceive, be admitted that cow-pox matter in the state now described may produce a disease, the effects of which may be felt both locally and generally, yet that the disease thus induced may not be effectual in obviating the future effects of variolous contagion. In the case of Mary Miller, related by Mr. Kite in the volume above alluded to, it appears that the inflammation and suppuration of the inoculated arm were more than usually severe, although the system underwent no specific change from the action of the virus; which appears from the patient's sickening seven weeks afterwards with the natural smallpox, which went through its course. Some of the cases communicated by Mr. Earle tend further to confirm this fact, as the matter there manifestly produced ulceration on the inoculated part to a considerable extent.

Fourthly. Whether the cow-pox is a spontaneous disease in the cow, or is to be attributed to matter conveyed to the animal, as I have conceived, from the horse, is a question which, though I shall not attempt now fully to discuss, yet I shall digress so far as to adduce some further observations, and to give my reasons more at large for taking up an opinion that to some had appeared fanciful. The aggregate of these observations, though not amounting to positive proof, forms presumptive evidence of so forcible a kind that I imagine it might, on any other person, have made the same impression it did on me, without fixing the imputation of credulity.

First: I conceived this was the source, from observing that where the cow-pox had appeared among the dairies here (unless it could be traced to the introduction of an infected cow or servant) it had been preceded at the farm by a horse diseased in the manner already described, which horse had been attended by some of the milkers.

Secondly: From its being a popular opinion throughout this great dairy country, and from its being insisted on by those who here attend sick cattle.

Thirdly: From the total absence of the disease in Ireland and Scotland, where the men-servants are not employed in the dairies.[4]

Fourthly: From having observed that morbid matter generated by the horse frequently communicates, in a casual way, a disease to the human subject so like the cow-pox that, in many cases, it would be difficult to make the distinction between one and the other.[5]

Fifthly: From being induced to suppose, from experiments, that some of those who had been thus affected from the horse resisted the smallpox.

Sixthly: From the progress and general appearance of the pustule on the arm of the boy whom I inoculated with matter taken from the hand of a man infected by a horse; and from the similarity to the cow-pox of general constitutional symptoms which followed.[6]

I fear it would be trespassing too far to adduce the general testimony of our farmers in support of this opinion; yet I beg leave to introduce an extract of a letter on this

[4] This information was communicated to me from the first authority.
[5] The sound skin does not appear to be susceptible of this virus when inserted into it, but, when previously diseased from little accidents, its effects are often conspicuous.
[6] This case (on which I laid no inconsiderable stress in my late treatise, as presumptive evidence of the fact adduced) seems to have been either mistaken or overlooked by those who have commented upon it. (See Case XVIII, p. 36.) The boy, unfortunately, died of a fever at a parish workhouse before I had an opportunity of observing what effects would have been produced by the matter of smallpox.

subject from the Rev. Mr. Moore, of Chalford Hill, in this county:

"In the month of November, 1797, my horse had diseased heels, which was certainly what is termed the grease; and at a short subsequent period my cow was also affected with what a neighbouring farmer (who was conversant with the complaints of cattle) pronounced to be the cow-pox, which he at the same time observed my servant would be infected with: and this proved to be the case; for he had eruptions on his hands, face, and many parts of the body, the pustules appearing large, and not much like the smallpox, for which he had been inoculated a year and a half before, and had then a very heavy burthen. The pustules on the face might arise from contact with his hands, as he had a habit of rubbing his forehead, where the sores were the largest and the thickest.

"The boy associated with the farmer's sons during the continuance of the disease, neither of whom had had the smallpox, but they felt no ill effects whatever. He was not much indisposed, as the disease did not prevent him from following his occupations as usual. No other person attended the horse or milked the cow but the lad above mentioned. I am firmly of opinion that the disease in the heels of the horse, which was a virulent grease, was the origin of the servant's and the cow's malady."

But to return to the more immediate object of this proposition.

From the similarity of symptoms, both constitutional and local, between the cow-pox and the disease received from morbid matter generated by a horse, the common people in this neighbourhood, when infected with this disease, through a strange perversion of terms, frequently call it the cow-pox. Let us suppose, then, such a malady to appear among some of the servants at a farm, and at the same time that the cow-pox were to break out among the cattle; and let us suppose, too, that some of the servants were infected in this way, and that others received the infection from the cows. It would be recorded at the farm, and among the servants themselves wherever they might afterwards be dispersed, that they had all had the cow-pox. But it is clear that an individual thus infected from the horse would neither be for a certainty secure himself, nor would he impart security to others were they inoculated by virus thus generated. He still would be in danger of taking the smallpox. Yet were this to happen before the nature of the cowpox be more maturely considered by the public my evidence on the subject might be depreciated unjustly. For an exemplification of what is here advanced relative to the nature of the infection when received directly from the horse see Inquiry into the Causes and Effects of the Variolæ Vaccinæ, pp. 27, 28, 29, 30, and p. 35; and by way of further example, I beg leave to subjoin the following intelligence received from Mr. Fewster, Surgeon, of Thornbury, in this county, a gentleman perfectly well acquainted with the appearances of the cow-pox on the human subject:

"William Morris, aged thirty-two, servant to Mr. Cox of Almondsbury, in this county, applied to me the 2d of April, 1798. He told me that, four days before, he found a stiffness and swelling in both his hands, which were so painful it was with difficulty he continued his work; that he had been seized with pain in his head, small of the back, and limbs, and with frequent chilly fits succeeded by fever. On examination I found him still affected with these symptoms, and that there was a great prostration of strength. Many parts of his hands on the inside were chapped, and on the middle joint of the thumb of the right hand there was a small phagedenic ulcer, about the size of a large pea, discharging an ichorous fluid. On the middle finger of the same hand there was another ulcer of a similar kind. These sores were of a *circular* form, and he described their first appearance as being somewhat like blisters arising from a burn. He complained of excessive pain, which extended up his arm into the axilla. These symptoms and appearances of the sores were so exactly like the cow-pox that I pronounced he had taken the distemper from milking cows. He assured me he had not milked a cow for more than half a year, and that his master's cows had nothing the matter with them. I then asked him if his master had a *greasy* horse, which he answered in the affirmative, and further said that he had constantly dressed him twice a day for the last three weeks or more, and remarked that the smell of his hands was much like that of the horses's heels. On the 5th of April I again saw him, and found him still complaining of pain in both hands, nor were his febrile symptoms at all relieved. The ulcers had now spread to the size of a seven-shilling gold coin, and another ulcer, which I had not noticed before, appeared on the first joint of the forefinger of the left hand, equally painful with that on the right. I ordered him to bathe his hands in warm bran and water, applied escharotics to the ulcers, and wrapped his hands up in a soft cataplasm. The next day he was much relieved, and in something more than a fortnight got well. He lost his nails from the thumb and fingers that were ulcerated."

The sudden disappearance of the symptoms in this case after the application of the escharotics to the sores is worthy of observation; it seems to show that they were kept up by the irritation of the ulcers.

The general symptoms which I have already described of the cow-pox, when communicated in a casual way to any great extent, will, I am convinced, from the many cases I have seen, be found accurate; but from the very slight indisposition which ensues in cases of inoculation, where the pustule, after affecting the constitution, quickly runs into a scab spontaneously, or is artificially suppressed by some proper application, I am induced to believe that the violence of the symptoms may be ascribed to the inflammation and irritation of the ulcers (when ulceration takes place to any extent, as in the casual cow-pox), and that the constitutional symptoms which appear during the presence of the sore, while it assumes the character of a pustule only, are felt but in a very trifling degree. This mild affection of the system happens when the disease makes but a slight local impression on those who have been accidentally infected by cows; and, as far as I have seen, it has uniformly happened among those who have been inoculated, when a pustule only and no great degree of inflammation or any ulceration has taken place from the inoculation. The following cases will strengthen this opinion.

The cow-pox appeared at a farm in the village of Stonehouse, in this county, about Michaelmas last, and continued gradually to pass from one cow to another till the end of November. On the twenty-sixth of that month some ichorous matter was taken from a cow and dried upon a quill. On the 2d of December some of it was inserted into a scratch, made so superficial that no blood appeared, on the arms of Susan Phipps, a child seven years old. The common inflammatory appearances took place in consequence, and advanced till the fifth day, when they had so much subsided that I did not conceive any thing further would ensue.

6th: Appearances stationary.

7th: The inflammation began to advance.

8th: A vesication, perceptible on the edges, forming, as in the inoculated smallpox, an appearance not unlike a grain of wheat, with the cleft, or indentation in the centre.

9th: Pain in the axilla.

10th: A little headache; pulse, 110; tongue not discoloured; countenance in health.

11th, 12th: No perceptible illness; pulse about 100.

13th: The pustule was now surrounded by an efflorescence, interspersed with very minute confluent pustules to the extent of about an inch. Some of these pustules advanced in size and maturated. So exact was the resemblance of the arm at this stage to the general appearance of the inoculated smallpox that Mr. D., a neighbouring surgeon, who took some matter from it, and who had never seen the cow-pox before, declared he could not perceive any difference.[7] The child's arm now shewed a disposition to scab, and remained nearly stationary for two or three days, when it began to run into an ulcerous state, and *then* commenced a febrile indisposition accompanied with an increase of axillary tumour. The ulcer continued spreading near a week, during which time the child continued ill, when

[7] That the cow-pox was a supposed guardian of the constitution from the action of the smallpox has been a prevalent idea for a long time past; but the similarity in the constitutional effects between one disease and the other could never have been so accurately observed had not the inoculation of the cow-pox placed it in a new and stronger point of view. This practice, too, has shewn us, what before lay concealed, the rise and progress of the pustule formed by the insertion of the virus, which places in a most conspicuous light its striking resemblance to the pustule formed from the inoculated smallpox.

it increased to a size nearly as large as a shilling. It began now to discharge pus; granulations sprang up, and it
healed. This child had before been of a remarkably sickly
constitution, but is now in very high health.

Mary Hearn, twelve years of age, was inoculated with
matter taken from the arm of Susan Phipps.

6th day: A pustule beginning to appear, slight pain in the
axilla.

7th: A distinct vesicle formed.

8th: The vesicle increasing; edges very red; no deviation
in its appearance at this time from the inoculated smallpox.

9th: No indisposition; pustule advancing.

10th: The patient felt this evening a slight febrile attack.

11th: Free from indisposition.

12th, 13th: The same.

14th: An efflorescence of a faint red colour extending
several inches round the arm. The pustule, beginning to
shew a disposition to spread, was dressed with an ointment
composed of *hydrarg. nit. rub. and ung. ceræ.* The efflorescence itself was covered with a plaster of *ung. hydr. fort.* In
six hours it was examined, when it was found that the
efflorescence had totally disappeared.

The application of the ointment with the *hydr. nit. rub.*
was made use of for three days, when, the state of the
pustule remaining stationary, it was exchanged for the *ung.
hydr. nit.* This appeared to have a more active effect than
the former, and in two or three days the virus seemed to be
subdued, when a simple dressing was made use of; but the
sore again shewing a disposition to inflame, the *ung. hydr.
nit.* was again applied, and soon answered the intended
purpose effectually. The girl, after the tenth day, when, as
has been observed, she became a little ill, shewed not the
least symptom of indisposition. She was afterwards exposed to the action of variolous matter, and completely resisted it. Susan Phipps also went through a similar trial.
Conceiving these cases to be important, I have given them
in detail: first, to urge the precaution of using such means
as may stop the progress of the pustule; and, secondly, to
point out (what appears to be the fact) that the most
material indisposition, or at least that which is felt most

sensibly, *does not arise primarily from the first action of the virus on the constitution, but that it often comes on, if the pustule is left to chance, as a secondary disease.* This leads me to conjecture, what experiment must finally determine, that they who have had the smallpox are not afterwards susceptible of the primary action of the cow-pox virus; for seeing that the simple virus itself, when it has not passed beyond the boundary of a vesicle, excites in the system so little commotion, is it not probable the trifling illness thus induced may be lost in that which so quickly, and oftentimes so severely, follows in the casual cow-pox from the presence of corroding ulcers? This consideration induces me to suppose that I may have been mistaken in my former observation on this subject.

In this respect, as well as many others, a parallel may be drawn between this disease and the smallpox. In the latter, the patient first feels the effect of what is called the absorption of the virus. The symptoms then often nearly retire, when a fresh attack commences, different from the first, and the illness keeps pace with the progress of the pustules through their different stages of maturation, ulceration, etc.

Although the application I have mentioned in the case of Mary Hearn proved sufficient to check the progress of ulceration and prevent any secondary symptoms, yet, after the pustule has duly exerted its influence, I should prefer the destroying it quickly and effectually to any other mode. The term caustic to a tender ear (and I conceive none feel more interested in this inquiry than the anxious guardians of a nursery) may sound harsh and unpleasing, but every solicitude that may arise on this account will no longer exist when it is understood that the pustule, in a state fit to be acted upon, is then quite superficial, and that it does not occupy the space of a silver penny.*

As a proof of the efficacy of this practice, even before the virus has fully exerted itself on the system, I shall lay before my reader the following history:

* I mention escharotics for stopping the progress of the pustule because I am acquainted with their efficacy; probably more simple means might answer the purpose quite as well, such as might be found among the mineral and vegetable astringents.

By a reference to the treatise on the Variolæ Vaccinæ
it will be seen that, in the month of April, 1798, four children were inoculated with the matter of cow-pox, and
that in two of these cases the virus on the arm was destroyed soon after it had produced a perceptible sickening.
Mary James, aged seven years, one of the children alluded
to, was inoculated in the month of December following with
fresh variolous matter, and at the same time was exposed
to the effluvia of a patient affected with the smallpox. The
appearance and progress of the infected arm was, in every
respect, similar to that which we generally observe when
variolous matter has been inserted into the skin of a person
who has not previously undergone either the cow-pox or the
smallpox. On the eighth day, conceiving there was infection in it, she was removed from her residence among
those who had not had the smallpox. I was now anxiously
waiting the result, conceiving, from the state of the girl's
arm, she would fall sick about this time. On visiting her
on the evening of the following day (the ninth) all I could
learn from the woman who attended her was that she felt
somewhat hotter than usual during the night, but was not
restless; and that in the morning there was the faint appearance of a rash about her wrists. This went off in a
few hours, and was not at all perceptible to me on my
visit in the evening. Not a single eruption appeared, the
skin having been repeatedly and carefully examined. The
inoculated arm continued to make the usual progress to the
end, through all the stages of inflammation, maturation, and
scabbing.

On the eighth day matter was taken from the arm of this
girl (Mary James) and inserted into the arms of her mother
and brother (neither of whom had had either the smallpox
or the cow-pox), the former about fifty years of age, the
latter six.

On the eighth day after the insertion the boy felt indisposed, and continued unwell two days, when a measles-like
rash appeared on his hands and wrists, and was thinly
scattered over his arms. The day following his body was
marbled over with an appearance somewhat similar, but he
did not complain, nor did he appear indisposed. A few

pustules now appeared, the greater part of which went away without maturing.

On the ninth day the mother began to complain. She was a little chilly and had a headache for two days, but *no pustule appeared on the skin,* nor had she any appearance of a rash.

The family was attended by an elderly woman as a nurse, who in her infancy had been exposed to the contagion of the smallpox, but had resisted it. This woman was now infected, but had the disease in the slightest manner, a very few eruptions appearing, two or three of which only maturated.

From a solitary instance like that adduced of Mary James, whose constitution appears to have resisted the action of the variolous virus, after the influence of the cow-pox virus had been so soon arrested in its progress, no positive conclusion can be fairly drawn; nor from the history of the three other patients who were subsequently infected, but, nevertheless, the facts collectively may be deemed interesting.

That one mild variety of the smallpox has appeared I have already plainly shewn;[9] and by the means now mentioned we probably have it in our power to produce at will another.

At the time when the pustule was destroyed in the arm of Mary James I was informed she had been indisposed about twelve hours; but I am now assured by those who were with her that the space of time was much less. Be that as it may, in cases of cow-pox inoculation I would not recommend any application to subdue the action of the pustule until convincing proofs had appeared of the patient's having felt its effects at least twelve hours. No harm, indeed, could ensue were a longer period to elapse before the application was made use of. In short, it should be suffered to have as full an effect as it could, consistently with the state of the arm.

As the cases of inoculation multiply, I am more and more convinced of the extreme mildness of the symptoms arising

[9] See Inquiry into the Causes and Effects of the Variolæ Vaccinæ, p. 54 (of original article).

merely from the primary action of the virus on the constitution, and that those symptoms which, as in the accidental cow-pox, affect the patient with severity, are entirely secondary, excited by the irritating processes of inflammation and ulceration; and it appears to me that this singular virus possesses an irritating quality of a peculiar kind, but as a single cow-pox pustule is all that is necessary to render the variolous virus ineffectual, and as we possess the means of allaying the irritation, should any arise, it becomes of little or no consequence.

It appears then, as far as an inference can be drawn from the present progress of cow-pox inoculation, that it is an accidental circumstance only which can render this a violent disease, and a circumstance of that nature which, fortunately, it is in the power of almost every one to avoid. I allude to the communication of the disease from cows. In this case, should the hands of the milker be affected with little accidental sores to any extent, every sore would become the nidus of infection and feel the influence of the virus; and the degree of violence in the constitutional symptoms would be in proportion to the number and to the state of these local affections. Hence it follows that a person, either by accident or design, might be so filled with these wounds from contact with the virus that the constitution might sink under the pressure.

Seeing that we possess the means of rendering the action of the sores mild, which, when left to chance, are capable of producing violent effects; and seeing, too, that these sores bear a resemblance to the smallpox, especially the confluent, should it not encourage the hope that some topical application might be used with advantage to counteract the fatal tendency of that disease, when it appears in this terrific form? At what stage or stages of the disease this may be done with the most promising expectation of success I will not pretend now to determine. I only throw out this idea as the basis of further reasoning and experiment.

I have often been foiled in my endeavours to communicate the cow-pox by inoculation. An inflammation will sometimes succeed the scratch or puncture, and in a few days disappear without producing any further effect. Sometimes it will even produce an ichorous fluid, and yet the system will not be affected. The same thing we know happens with the smallpox virus.

Four or five servants were inoculated at a farm contiguous to this place, last summer, with matter just taken from an infected cow. A little inflammation appeared on all their arms, but died away without producing a pustule; yet all these servants caught the disease within a month afterwards from milking the infected cows, and some of them had it severely. At present no other mode than that commonly practiced for inoculating the smallpox has been used for giving the cow-pox; but it is probable this might be varied with advantage. We should imitate the casual communication more clearly were we first, by making the smallest superficial incision or puncture on the skin, to produce a little scab, and then, removing it, to touch the abraded part with the virus. A small portion of a thread imbrued in the virus (as in the old method of inoculating the smallpox) and laid upon the slightly incised skin might probably prove a successful way of giving the disease; or the cutis might be exposed in a minute point by an atom of blistering plaster, and the virus brought in contact with it. In the cases just alluded to, where I did not succeed in giving the disease constitutionally, the experiment was made with matter taken in a purulent state from a pustule on the nipple of a cow.

Is *pure pus,* though contained in a smallpox pustule, ever capable of producing the smallpox perfectly? I suspect it is not. Let us consider that it is always preceded by the limpid fluid, which, in constitutions susceptible of variolous contagion, is always infectious; and though, on opening a pustule, its contents may appear perfectly purulent, yet a given quantity of the limpid fluid may, at the same time, be blended with it, though it would be imperceptible to the only test of our senses, the eye. The presence, then, of this fluid, or its mechanical diffusion through pus, may at all times render active what is apparently *mere pus,* while its total absence (as in stale pustules) may be attended with the imperfect effects we have seen.

It would be digressing too widely to go far into the

doctrine of secretion, but as it will not be quite extraneous, I shall just observe that I consider both the pus and the limpid fluid of the pustule as secretions, but that the organs established by nature to perform the office of secreting these fluids may differ essentially in their mechanical structure. What but a difference in the organization of glandular bodies constitutes the difference in the qualities of the fluids secreted? From some peculiar derangement in the structure or, in other words, some deviation in the natural action of a gland destined to create a mild, innoxious fluid, a poison of the most deadly nature may be created; for example: That gland, which in its sound state secretes pure saliva, may, from being thrown into diseased action, produce a poison of the most destructive quality. Nature appears to have no more difficulty in forming minute glands among the vascular parts of the body than she has in forming blood vessels, and millions of these can be called into existence, when inflammation is excited, in a few hours.[10]

In the present early stage of the inquiry (for early it certainly must be deemed), before we know for an absolute certainty how soon the virus of the cow-pox may suffer a change in its specific properties, after it has quitted the limpid state it possesses when forming a pustule, it would be prudent for those who have been inoculated with it to submit to variolous inoculation. No injury or inconvenience can accrue from this; and were the same method practiced among those who, from inoculation, have felt the smallpox in an unsatisfactory manner at any period of their lives, it might appear that I had not been too officious in offering a cautionary hint in recommending a second inoculation with matter in its most perfect state.

And here let me suppose, for argument's sake (not from conviction), that one person in an hundred after having had the cow-pox should be found susceptible of the smallpox, would this invalidate the utility of the practice? For, waiving all other considerations, who will deny that the inoculated smallpox, although abstractedly it may be considered as

[10] Mr. Home, in his excellent dissertation on pus and mucus, justifies this assertion.

harmless, does not involve in itself something that in number-less instances proves baneful to the human frame.

That in delicate constitutions it sometimes excites scrofula is a fact that must generally be subscribed to, as it is so obvious to common observation. This consideration is important.

As the effects of the smallpox inoculation on those who have had the cow-pox will be watched with the most scrupulous eye by those who prosecute this inquiry, it may be proper to bring to their recollection some facts relative to the smallpox, which I must consider here as of consequence, but which hitherto seem not to have made a due impression.

It should be remembered that the constitution cannot, by previous infection, be rendered totally unsusceptible of the variolous poison; neither the casual nor the inoculated small-pox, whether it produces the disease in a mild or in a violent way, can perfectly extinguish the susceptibility. The skin, we know, is ever ready to exhibit, though often in a very limited degree, the effects of the poison when inserted there; and how frequently do we see, among nurses, when much exposed to the contagion, eruptions, and these sometimes preceded by sensible illness! yet should any thing like an eruption appear, or the smallest degree of indisposition, upon the insertion of the variolous matter on those who have gone through the cow-pox, my assertions respecting the peculiarities of the disease might be unjustly discredited.

I know a gentleman who, many years ago, was inoculated for the smallpox, but having no pustules, or scarcely any constitutional affection that was perceptible, he was dissatisfied, and has since been repeatedly inoculated. A vesicle has always been produced in the arm in consequence, with axillary swelling and a slight indisposition; this is by no means a rare occurrence. It is probable that fluid thus excited upon the skin would always produce the smallpox.

On the arm of a person who had gone through the cow-pox many years before I once produced a vesication by the insertion of variolous matter, and, with a little of the fluid, inoculated a young woman who had a mild, but very efficacious, smallpox in consequence, although no constitutional effect was produced on the patient from whom the matter was taken. The following communication from Mr. Fewster affords a still clearer elucidation of this fact. Mr. Fewster says: "On the 3d of April, 1797, I inoculated Master H——, aged fourteen months, for the smallpox. At the usual time he sickened, had a plentiful eruption, particularly on his face, and got well. His nursemaid, aged twenty-four, had many years before gone through the smallpox, in the natural way, which was evident from her being much pitted with it. She had used the child to sleep on her left arm, with her left cheek in contact with his face, and during his inoculation he had mostly slept in that manner. About a week after the child got well she (the nurse) desired me to look at her face, which she said was very painful. There was a plentiful eruption on the left cheek, *but not on any other part of the body,* which went on to maturation.

"On enquiry I found that three days before the appearance of the eruption she was taken with slight chilly fits, pain in her head and limbs, and some fever. On the appearance of the eruption these pains went off, and now, the second day of the eruption, she complains of a little sore throat. Whether the above symptoms are the effects of the smallpox or a recent cold I do not know. On the fifth day of the eruption I charged a lancet from two of the pustules, and on the next day I inoculated two children, one two years, the other four months old, with the matter. At the same time I inoculated the mother and eldest sister with variolous matter taken from Master H——. On the fifth day of their inoculation *all* their arms were inflamed alike; and on the eighth day the eldest of those inoculated from the nurse sickened, and the youngest on the eleventh. They had both a plentiful eruption, from which I inoculated several others, who had the disease very favourably. The mother and the other child sickened about the same time, and likewise had a plentiful eruption.

"Soon after, a man in the village sickened with the smallpox and had a confluent kind. To be convinced that the children had had the disease effectually I took them to his house and inoculated them in both arms with matter taken from him, but without effect."

These are not brought forward as uncommon occurrences,

but as exemplifications of the human system's susceptibility of the variolous contagion, although it has been previously sensible of its action.

Happy is it for mankind that the appearance of the small-pox a second time on the same person, beyond a trivial extent, is so extremely rare that it is looked upon as a phænomenon! Indeed, since the publication of Dr. Heber-den's paper on the *Varicellæ*, or chicken-pox, the idea of such an occurrence, in deference to authority so truly respectable, has been generally relinquished. This I conceive has been without just reason; for after we have seen, among many others, so strong a case as that recorded by Mr. Edward Withers, Surgeon, of Newbury, Berks, in the fourth volume of the Memoirs of the Medical Society of London (from which I take the following extracts), no one, I think, will again doubt the fact.

"Mr. Richard Langford, a farmer of West Shefford, in this county (Berks), about fifty years of age, when about a month old had the smallpox at a time when three others of the family had the same disease, one of whom, a servant man, died of it. Mr. Langford's countenance was strongly indicative of the malignity of the distemper, his face being so remarkably pitted and seamed as to attract the notice of all who saw him, so that no one could entertain a doubt of his having had that disease in a most inveterate manner." Mr. Withers proceeds to state that Mr. Langford was seized a second time, had a bad confluent smallpox, and died on the twenty-first day from the seizure; and that four of the family, as also a sister of the patient's, to whom the disease was conveyed by her son's visiting his uncle, falling down with the smallpox, fully satisfied the country with regard to the nature of the disease, which nothing short of this would have done; the sister died.

"This case was thought so extraordinary a one as to in-duce the rector of the parish to record the particulars in the parish register."

It is singular that in most cases of this kind the disease in the first instance has been confluent; so that the extent of the ulceration on the skin (as in the cow-pox) is not the process in nature which affords security to the constitution.

As the subject of the smallpox is so interwoven with that which is the more immediate object of my present concern, it must plead my excuse for so often introducing it. At present it must be considered as a distemper not well understood. The inquiry I have instituted into the nature of the cowpox will probably promote its more perfect investigation.

The inquiry of Dr. Pearson into the history of the cow-pox having produced so great a number of attestations in favour of my assertion that it proves a protection to the human body from the smallpox, I have not been assiduous in seeking for more; but as some of my friends have been so good as to communicate the following, I shall conclude these observations with their insertion.

Extract of a letter from Mr. Drake, Surgeon, at Stroud, in this county, and late Surgeon to the North Gloucester Regiment of Militia:

"In the spring of the year 1796 I inoculated men, women, and children to the amount of about seventy. Many of the men did not receive the infection, although inoculated at least three times and kept in the same room with those who actually underwent the disease during the whole time occupied by them in passing through it. Being anxious they should, in future, be secure against it, I was very particular in my inquiries to find out whether they ever had previously had it, or at any time been in the neighbourhood of people labouring under it. But, after all, the only satisfactory information I could obtain was that they had had the cow-pox. As I was then ignorant of such a disease affecting the human subject, I flattered myself what they imagined to be the cowpox was in reality the smallpox in a very slight degree. I mentioned the circumstance in the presence of the officers, at the time expressing my doubts if it were not smallpox, and was not a little surprised when I was told by the Colonel that he had frequently heard you mention the cow-pox as a disease endemial to Gloucestershire, and that if a person were ever affected by it, you supposed him afterwards secure from the smallpox. This excited my curiosity, and when I visited Gloucestershire I was very inquisitive concerning the subject, and from the information I have since received, both from your publication and from conversation with medical men of the greatest accuracy in their observations, I am fully convinced that what the men supposed to be cow-pox was actually so, and I can safely affirm that they effectually resisted the smallpox."

Mr. Fry, Surgeon, at Dursley in this county, favours me with the following communication:

"During the spring of the year 1797 I inoculated fourteen hundred and seventy-five patients, of all ages, from a fortnight old to seventy years; amongst whom there were many who had previously gone through the cow-pox. The exact number I cannot state; but if I say there were nearly thirty, I am certainly within the number. There was not a single instance of the variolous matter producing any constitutional effect on these people, nor any greater degree of local inflammation than it would have done in the arm of a person who had before gone through the smallpox, notwithstanding it was invariably inserted four, five, and sometimes six different times, to satisfy the minds of the patients. In the common course of inoculation previous to the general one scarcely a year passed without my meeting with one or two instances of persons who had gone through the cow-pox, resisting the action of the variolous contagion. I may fairly say that the number of people I have seen inoculated with the smallpox who, at former periods, had gone through the cow-pox, are not less than forty; and in no one instance have I known a patient receive the smallpox, notwithstanding they invariably continued to associate with other inoculated patients during the progress of the disease, and many of them purposely exposed themselves to the contagion of the natural smallpox; whence I am fully convinced that a person who had *fairly* had the cow-pox is no longer capable of being acted upon by the variolous matter.

"I also inoculated a very considerable number of those who had had a disease which ran through the neighbourhood a few years ago, and was called by the common people the *swine-pox*, not one of whom received the smallpox."[11]

"There were about half a dozen instances of people who never had either the cow- or swine-pox, yet did not receive

[11] This was that mild variety of the smallpox which I have noticed in the late Treatise on the Cow-Pox (p. 233).

the smallpox, the system not being in the least deranged, or
the arms inflamed, although they were repeatedly inoculated,
and associated with others who were labouring under the
disease; one of them was the son of a farrier."

Mr. Tierny, Assistant Surgeon of the South Gloucester
Regiment of Militia, has obliged me with the following information:

"That in the summer of the year of 1798 he inoculated a
great number of the men belonging to the regiment, and that
among them he found eleven who, from having lived in
dairies, had gone through the cow-pox. That all of them
resisted the smallpox except one, but that on making the most
rigid and scrupulous enquiry at the farm in Gloucestershire,
where the man said he lived when he had the disease, and
among those with whom, at the same time, he declared he
had associated, and particularly of a person in the parish,
whom he said had dressed his fingers, it most clearly appeared
that he aimed at an imposition, and that he never had been
affected with the cow-pox."[12] Mr. Tierny remarks that the
arms of many who were inoculated after having had the
cow-pox inflamed very quickly, and that in several a little
ichorous fluid was formed.

Mr. Cline, who in July last was so obliging at my request
as to try the efficacy of the cow-pox virus, was kind enough
to give me a letter on the result of it, from which the following is an extract:

"MY DEAR SIR:
"The cow-pox experiment has succeeded admirably. The
child sickened on the seventh day, and the fever, which was
moderate, subsided on the eleventh. The inflammation arising from the insertion of the virus extended to about four
inches in diameter, and then gradually subsided, without having been attended with pain or other inconvenience. There
were no eruptions.

"I have since inoculated him with smallpox matter in three
places, which were slightly inflamed on the third day, and
then subsided.

[12] The public cannot be too much upon their guard respecting persons of
this description.

"Dr. Lister, who was formerly physician to the Smallpox Hospital, attended the child with me, and he is convinced that it is not possible to give him the smallpox. I think the substituting the cow-pox poison for the smallpox promises to be one of the greatest improvements that has ever been made in medicine; and the more I think on the subject, the more I am impressed with its importance.

"With great esteem
"I am, etc.,
"HENRY CLINE.

"Lincoln's Inn Fields,
    August 2, 1798."

From communications, with which I have been favoured from Dr. Pearson, who has occasionally reported to me the result of his private practice with the vaccine virus in London, and from Dr. Woodville, who also has favoured me with an account of his more extensive inoculation with the same virus at the Smallpox Hospital, it appears that many of their patients have been affected with eruptions, and that these eruptions have maturated in a manner very similar to the variolous. The matter they made use of was taken in the first instance from a cow belonging to one of the great milk farms in London. Having never seen maturated pustules produced either in my own practice among those who were casually infected by cows, or those to whom the disease had been communicated by inoculation, I was desirous of seeing the effect of the matter generated in London, on subjects living in the country. A thread imbrued in some of this matter was sent to me, and with it two children were inoculated, whose cases I shall transcribe from my notes.

Stephen Jenner, three years and a half old.

3d day: The arm shewed a proper and decisive inflammation.

6th: A vesicle arising.

7th: The pustule of a cherry colour.

8th: Increasing in elevation. A few spots now appear on each arm near the insertion of the inferior tendons of the biceps muscles. They are very small and of a vivid red colour. The pulse natural; tongue of its natural hue; no loss of appetite or any symptom of indisposition.

9th: The inoculated pustule on the arm this evening began to inflame, and gave the child uneasiness; he cried and pointed to the seat of it, and was immediately afterwards affected with febrile symptoms. At the expiration of two hours after the seizure a plaster of *ung. hydrarg. fort.* was applied, and its effect was very quickly perceptible, for in ten minutes he resumed his usual looks and playfulness. On examining the arm about three hours after the application of the plaster its effects in subduing the inflammation were very manifest.

10th: The spots on the arms have disappeared, but there are three visible in the face.

11th: Two spots on the face are gone; the other barely percе́ tible.

13th: The pustule delineated in the second plate in the Treatise on the Variolæ Vaccinæ is a correct representation of that on the child's arm as it appears at this time.

14th: Two fresh spots appear on the face. The pustule on the arm nearly converted into a scab. As long as any fluid remained in it it was limpid.

James Hill, four years old, was inoculated on the same day, and with part of the same matter which infected Stephen Jenner. It did not appear to have taken effect till the fifth day.

7th: A perceptible vesicle: this evening the patient became a little chilly; no pain or tumour discoverable in the axilla.

8th: Perfectly well.

9th: The same.

10th: The vesicle more elevated than I have been accustomed to see it, and assuming more perfectly the variolous character than is common with the cow-pox at this stage.

11th: Surrounded by an inflammatory redness, about the size of a shilling, studded over with minute vesicles. The pustule contained a limpid fluid till the fourteenth day, after which it was incrusted over in the usual manner; but this incrustation or scab being accidentally rubbed off, it was slow in healing.

These children were afterwards fully exposed to the smallpox contagion without effect.

Having been requested by my friend, Mr. Henry Hicks, of Eastington, in this county, to inoculate two of his children, and at the same time some of his servants and the people employed in his manufactory, matter was taken from the arm of this boy for the purpose. The numbers inoculated were eighteen. They all took the infection, and either on the fifth or sixth day a vesicle was perceptible on the punctured part. Some of them began to feel a little unwell on the eighth day, but the greater number on the ninth. Their illness, as in the former cases described, was of short duration, and not sufficient to interrupt, but at very short intervals, the children from their amusements, or the servants and manufacturers from following their ordinary business.

Three of the children whose employment in the manufactory was in some degree laborious had an inflammation on their arms beyond the common boundary about the eleventh or twelfth day, when the feverish symptoms, which before were nearly gone off, again returned, accompanied with increase of axillary tumour. In these cases (clearly perceiving that the symptoms were governed by the state of the arms) I applied on the inoculated pustules, and renewed the application three or four times within an hour, a pledget of lint, previously soaked in *aqua lythargyri acetati*,[13] and covered the hot efflorescence surrounding them with cloths dipped in cold water.

The next day I found this simple mode of treatment had succeeded perfectly. The inflammation was nearly gone off, and with it the symptoms which it had produced.

Some of these patients have since been inoculated with variolous matter, without any effect beyond a little inflammation on the part where it was inserted.

Why the arms of those inoculated with the vaccine matter in the country should be more disposed to inflame than those inoculated in London it may be difficult to determine. From comparing my own cases with some transmitted to

[13] Goulard's extract of Saturn.

me by Dr. Pearson and Dr. Woodville, this appears to be the fact; and what strikes me as still more extraordinary with respect to those inoculated in London is the appearance of maturating eruptions. In the two instances only which I have mentioned (the one from the inoculated, the other from the casual, cow-pox) a few red spots appeared, which quickly went off without maturating. The case of the Rev. Mr. Moore's servant may, indeed, seem like a deviation from the common appearances in the country, but the nature of these eruptions was not ascertained beyond their not possessing the property of communicating the disease by their effluvia. Perhaps the difference we perceive may be owing to some variety in the mode of action of the virus upon the skin of those who breathe the air of London and those who live in the country. That the erysipelas assumes a different form in London from what we see it put on in this country is a fact very generally acknowledged. In calling the inflammation that is excited by the cow-pox virus erysipelatous, perhaps I may not be critically exact, but it certainly approaches near to it. Now, as the diseased action going forward in the part infected with the virus may undergo different modifications according to the peculiarities of the constitution on which it is to produce its effect, may it not account for the variation which has been observed?

To this it may probably be objected that some of the patients inoculated, and who had pustules in consequence, were newly come from the country; but I conceive that the changes wrought in the human body through the medium of the lungs may be extremely rapid. Yet, after all, further experiments made in London with vaccine virus generated in the country must finally throw a light on what now certainly appears obscure and mysterious.

The principal variation perceptible to me in the action of the vaccine virus generated in London from that produced in the country was its proving more certainly infectious and giving a less disposition in the arm to inflame. There appears also a greater elevation of the pustule above the surrounding skin. In my former cases the pustule produced by the insertion of the virus was more like one of those which are so thickly spread over the body in a bad kind of confluent smallpox. This was more like a pustule of the distinct smallpox, except that I saw no instance of pus being formed in it, the matter remaining limpid till the period of scabbing.

Wishing to see the effects of the disease on an infant newly born, my nephew, Mr. Henry Jenner, at my request, inserted the vaccine virus into the arm of a child about twenty hours old. His report to me is that the child went through the disease without apparent illness, yet that it was found effectually to resist the action of variolous matter with which it was subsequently inoculated.

I have had an opportunity of trying the effects of the cow-pox matter on a boy, who, the day preceding its insertion, sickened with the measles. The eruption of the measles, attended with cough, a little pain in the chest, and the usual symptoms accompanying the disease, appeared on the third day and spread all over him. The disease went through its course without any deviation from its usual habits; and, notwithstanding this, the cow-pox virus excited its common appearances, both on the arm and on the constitution, without any febrile interruption; on the sixth day there was a vesicle.

8th: Pain in the axilla, chilly, and affected with headache.

9th: Nearly well.

12th: The pustule spread to the size of a large split-pea, but without any surrounding efflorescence. It soon afterwards scabbed, and the boy recovered his general health rapidly. But it should be observed that before it scabbed the efflorescence which had suffered a temporary suspension advanced in the usual manner.

Here we see a deviation from the ordinary habits of the smallpox, as it has been observed that the presence of the measles suspends the action of the variolous matter.

The very general investigation that is now taking place, chiefly through inoculation (and I again repeat my earnest hope that it may be conducted with that calmness and moderation which should ever accompany a philosophical research), must soon place the vaccine disease in its just point of view. The result of all my trials with the virus

(14) HC XXXVIII

on the human subject has been uniform. In every instance
the patient who has felt its influence, has completely lost
the susceptibility for the variolous contagion; and as these
instances are now become numerous, I conceive that, joined
to the observations in the former part of this paper, they
sufficiently preclude me from the necessity of entering into
controversies with those who have circulated reports adverse to my assertions, on no other evidence than what
has been casually collected.

III

A CONTINUATION OF FACTS AND OBSERVATIONS RELATIVE TO THE VARIOLÆ VACCINÆ, OR COW-POX. 1800

SINCE my former publications on the vaccine inoculation
I have had the satisfaction of seeing it extend very widely.
Not only in this country is the subject pursued with ar-
dour, but from my correspondence with many respectable
medical gentlemen on the Continent (among whom are Dr.
De Carro, of Vienna, and Dr. Ballhorn, of Hanover) I
find it is as warmly adopted abroad, where it has afforded
the greatest satisfaction. I have the pleasure, too, of seeing that the feeble efforts of a few individuals to depreciate
the new practice are sinking fast into contempt beneath
the immense mass of evidence which has arisen up in
support of it.

Upwards of six thousand persons have now been inoculated with the virus of cow-pox, and the far greater part
of them have since been inoculated with that of smallpox, and exposed to its infection in every rational way
that could be devised, without effect.

It was very improbable that the investigation of a
disease so analogous to the smallpox should go forward
without engaging the attention of the physician of the
Smallpox Hospital in London.

Accordingly, Dr. Woodville, who fills that department
with so much respectability, took an early opportunity
of instituting an inquiry into the nature of the cow-pox.
This inquiry was begun in the early part of the present
year, and in May, Dr. Woodville published the result,

which differs essentially from mine in a point of much importance. It appears that three-fifths of the patients inoculated were affected with eruptions, for the most part so perfectly resembling the smallpox as not to be distinguished from them. On this subject it is necessary that I should make some comments.

When I consider that out of the great number of cases of casual inoculation immediately from cows which from time to time presented themselves to my observation, and the many similar instances which have been communicated to me by medical gentlemen in this neighbourhood; when I consider, too, that the matter with which my inoculations were conducted in the years 1797, '98, and '99, was taken from some different cows, and that in no instance any thing like a variolous pustule appeared, I cannot feel disposed to imagine that eruptions, similar to those described by Dr. Woodville, have ever been produced by the *pure uncontaminated cow-pock virus;* on the contrary, I do suppose that those which the doctor speaks of originated in the action of variolous matter which crept into the constitution with the vaccine. And this I presume happened from the inoculation of a great number of the patients with variolous matter (some on the third, others on the fifth, day) after the vaccine had been applied; and it should be observed that the matter thus propagated became the source of future inoculations in the hands of many medical gentlemen who appeared to have been previously unacquainted with the nature of the cow-pox.

Another circumstance strongly, in my opinion, supporting this supposition is the following: The cow-pox has been known among our dairies time immemorial. If pustules, then, like the variolous, were to follow the communication of it from the cow to the milker, would not such a fact have been known and recorded at our farms? Yet neither our farmers nor the medical people of the neighbourhood have noticed such an occurrence.

A few scattered pimples I have sometimes, though very rarely, seen, the greater part of which have generally disappeared quickly, but some have remained long enough to suppurate at their apex. That local cuticular inflam-

mation, whether springing up spontaneously or arising
from the application of acrid substances, such for instance,
as *cantharides, pix Burgundica, antimonium tartarizatum,*
etc., will often produce cutaneous affections, not only near
the seat of the inflammation, but on some parts of the
skin far beyond its boundary, is a well-known fact. It is,
doubtless, on this principle that the inoculated cow-pock
pustule and its concomitant efflorescence may, in very ir-
ritable constitutions, produce this affection. The eruption
I allude to has commonly appeared some time in the third
week after inoculation. But this appearance is too trivial
to excite the least regard.

The change which took place in the general appearance during the progress of the vaccine inoculation at the
Smallpox Hospital should likewise be considered.

Although at first it took on so much of the variolous
character as to produce pustules in three cases out of
five, yet in Dr. Woodville's last report, published in June,
he says: "Since the publication of my reports of inoculations for the cow-pox, upwards of three hundred cases
have been under my care; and out of this number only
thirty-nine had pustules that suppurated; viz., out of the
first hundred, nineteen had pustules; out of the second,
thirteen; and out of the last hundred and ten, only seven
had pustules. Thus it appears that the disease has become considerably milder; which I am inclined to attribute
to a greater caution used in the choice of the matter, with
which the infection was communicated; for, lately, that
which has been employed for this purpose has been taken
only from those patients in whom the cow-pox proved
very mild and well characterized."[1]

The inference I am induced to draw from these premises
is very different. The decline, and, finally, the total extinction nearly, of these pustules, in my opinion, are more
fairly attributable to the cow-pox virus, assimilating the
variolous,[2] the former probably being the original, the lat-

[1] In a few weeks after the cow-pox inoculation was introduced at the
Smallpox Hospital I was favoured with some virus from this stock. In the
first instance it produced a few pustules, which did not maturate; but in
the subsequent cases none appeared.—E. J.
[2] In my first publication on this subject I expressed an opinion that the
smallpox and the cow-pox were the same diseases under different modifica-

ter the same disease under a peculiar, and at present an inexplicable, modification.

One experiment tending to elucidate the point under discussion I had myself an opportunity of instituting. On the supposition of its being possible that the cow which ranges over the fertile meadows in the vale of Gloucester might generate a virus differing in some respects in its qualities from that produced by the animal artificially pampered for the production of milk for the metropolis, I procured, during my residence there in the spring, some cow pock virus from a cow at one of the London milk-farms.[a] It was immediately conveyed into Gloucestershire to Dr. Marshall, who was then extensively engaged in the inoculation of the cow-pox, the general result of which, and of the inoculation in particular with this matter, I shall lay before my reader in the following communication from the doctor:

" DEAR SIR:

" My neighbour, Mr. Hicks, having mentioned your wish to be informed of the progress of the inoculation here for the cow-pox, and he also having taken the trouble to transmit to you my minutes of the cases which have fallen under my care, I hope you will pardon the further trouble I now give you in stating the observations I have made upon the subject. When first informed of it, having two children who had not had the smallpox, I determined to inoculate them for the cow-pox whenever I should be so fortunate as to procure matter proper for the purpose. I was, therefore, particularly happy when I was informed that I could procure matter from some of those whom you had inoculated. In the first instance I had no intention of extending the disease further than my own family, but the very extensive influence which the conviction of its efficacy in resisting the smallpox has had upon the minds of the people in general has rendered that intention nugatory, as

tions. In this opinion Dr. Woodville has concurred. The axiom of the immortal Hauter, that *two diseased actions cannot take place at the same time in one and the same part*, will not be injured by the admission of this theory.
[a] It was taken by Mr. Tanner, then a student at the Veterinary College, from a cow at Mr. Clark's farm at Kentish Town.

you will perceive, by the continuation of my cases enclosed in this letter,[4] by which it will appear that since the 22d of March I have inoculated an hundred and seven persons; which, considering the retired situation I resided in, is a very great number. There are also other considerations which, besides that of its influence in resisting the small-pox, appear to have had their weight; the peculiar mild-ness of the disease, the known safety of it, and its not having in any instance prevented the patient from fol-lowing his ordinary business. In all the cases under my care there have only occurred two or three which required any application, owing to erysipelatous inflammation on the arm, and they immediately yielded to it. In the re-mainder the constitutional illness has been slight but suf-ficiently marked, and considerably less than I ever ob-served in the same number inoculated with the smallpox. In only one or two of the cases have any other eruptions appeared than those around the spot where the matter was inserted, and those near the infected part. Neither does there appear in the cow-pox to be the least exciting cause to any other disease, which in the smallpox has been frequently observed, the constitution remaining in as full health and vigour after the termination of the disease as before the infection. Another important consideration ap-pears to be the impossibility of the disease being com-municated except by the actual contact of the matter of the pustule, and consequently the perfect safety of the re-maining part of the family, supposing only one or two should wish to be inoculated at the same time.

"Upon the whole, it appears evident to me that the cow-pox is a pleasanter, shorter, and infinitely more safe disease than the inoculated smallpox when conducted in the most careful and approved manner; neither is the local affection of the inoculated part, or the constitutional ill-ness, near so violent. I speak with confidence on the sub-ject, having had an opportunity of observing its effects upon a variety of constitutions, from three months old to sixty years; and to which I have paid particular at-

[4] Doctor Marshall has detailed these cases with great accuracy, but their publication would now be deemed superfluous.—E. J.

tention. In the cases alluded to here you will observe that the removal from the original source of the matter had made no alteration or change in the nature or appearance of the disease, and that it may be continued, *ad infinitum* (I imagine), from one person to another (if care be observed in taking the matter at a proper period) without any necessity of recurring to the original matter of the cow.

"I should be happy if any endeavours of mine could tend further to elucidate the subject, and shall be much gratified is sending you any further observations I may be enabled to make.

"I have the pleasure to subscribe myself,

"Dear sir, etc.,

"Joseph H. Marshall.

"Eastington, Gloucestershire, April 26, 1799."

The gentleman who favoured me with the above account has continued to prosecute his inquiries with unremitting industry, and has communicated the result in another letter, which at his request I lay before the public without abbreviation.

Dr. Marshall's second letter:

"Dear Sir:

"Since the date of my former letter I have continued to inoculate with the cow-pox virus. Including the cases before enumerated, the number now amounts to four hundred and twenty-three. It would be tedious and useless to detail the progress of the disease in each individual—it is sufficient to observe that I noticed no deviation in any respect from the cases I formerly adduced. The general appearances of the arm exactly corresponded with the account given in your first publication. When they were disposed to become troublesome by erysipelatous inflammation, an application of equal parts of vinegar and water always answered the desired intention. I must not omit to inform you that when the disease had duly acted upon the constitution I have frequently used the vitriolic acid. A portion of a drop applied with the head of a probe or any convenient utensil upon the pustule, suffered to remain about forty seconds, and afterwards washed off with sponge and water, never failed to stop its progress and expedite the formation of a scab.

"I have already subjected two hundred and eleven of my patients to the action of variolous matter, *but every one resisted it.*

"The result of my experiments (which were made with every requisite caution) has fully convinced me that the *true cow-pox* is a safe and infallible preventive from the smallpox; that in no case which has fallen under my observation has it been in any considerable degree troublesome, much less have I seen any thing like danger; for in no instance were the patients prevented from following their ordinary employments.

"In Dr. Woodville's publication on the cow-pox I notice an extraordinary fact. He says that the generality of his patients had pustules. It certainly appears extremely extraordinary that in all my cases there never was but one pustule, which appeared on a patient's elbow on the inoculated arm, and maturated. It appeared exactly like that on the incised part.

"The whole of my observations, founded as it appears on an extensive experience, leads me to these obvious conclusions; that those cases which have been or may be adduced against the preventive powers of the cow-pox could not have been those of the true kind, since it must appear to be absolutely impossible that I should have succeeded in such a number of cases without a single exception if such a preventive power did not exist. I cannot entertain a doubt that the inoculated cow-pox must quickly supersede that of the smallpox. If the many important advantages which must result from the new practice are duly considered, we may reasonably infer that public benefit, the sure test of the real merit of discoveries, will render it generally extensive.

"To you, Sir, as the discoverer of this highly beneficial practice, mankind are under the highest obligations. As a private individual I participate in the general feeling; more particularly as you have afforded me an opportunity of noticing the effects of a singular disease, and of viewing the progress of the most curious experiment that ever was recorded in the history of physiology.

"I remain, dear sir, etc.,

"JOSEPH H. MARSHALL."

"P.S. I should have observed that, of the patients I inoculated and enumerated in my letter, one hundred and twenty-seven were infected with the matter you sent me from the London cow. I discovered no dissimilarity of symptoms in these cases from those which I inoculated from matter procured in this country. No pustules have occurred, except in one or two cases, where a single one appeared on the inoculated arm. No difference was apparent in the local inflammation. There was no suspension of ordinary employment among the labouring people, nor was any medicine required.

"I have frequently inoculated one or two in a family, and the remaining part of it some weeks afterwards. The uninfected have slept with the infected during the whole course of the disease without being affected; so that I am fully convinced that the disease cannot be taken but by actual contact with the matter.

"A curious fact has lately fallen under my observation, on which I leave you to comment.

"I visited a patient with the confluent smallpox and charged a lancet with some of the matter. Two days afterwards I was desired to inoculate a woman and four children with the cow-pox, and I inadvertently took the vaccine matter on the same lancet which was before charged with that of smallpox. In three days I discovered the mistake, and fully expected that my five patients would be infected with smallpox; but I was agreeably surprised to find the disease to be genuine cow-pox, which proceeded without deviating in any particular from my former cases. I afterwards inoculated these patients with variolous matter, but all of them resisted its action.

"I omitted mentioning another great advantage that now occurs to me in the inoculated cow-pox; I mean the safety with which pregnant women may have the disease communicated to them. I have inoculated a great number of females in that situation, and never observed their cases to differ in any respect from those of my other patients. Indeed, the disease is so mild that it seems as if it might at all times be communicated with the most perfect safety."

I shall here take the oportunity of thanking Dr. Marshall and those other gentlemen who have obligingly presented me with the result of their inoculations; but, as they all agree in the same point as that given in the above communication, namely, the security of the patient from the effects of the smallpox after the cow-pox, their perusal, I presume, would afford us no satisfaction that has not been amply given already. Particular occurrences I shall, of course, detail. Some of my correspondents have mentioned the appearance of smallpox-like eruptions at the commencement of their inoculations; but in these cases the matter was derived from the original stock at the Smallpox Hospital.

I have myself inoculated a very considerable number from the matter produced by Dr. Marshall's patients, originating in the London cow, without observing pustules of any kind, and have dispersed it among others who have used it with a similar effect. From this source Mr. H. Jenner informs me he has inoculated above an hundred patients without observing eruptions. Whether the nature of the virus will undergo any change from being farther removed from its original source in passing successively from one person to another time alone can determine. That which I am now employing has been in use near eight months, and not the least change is perceptible in its mode of action either locally or constitutionally. There is, therefore, every reason to expect that its effects will remain unaltered and that we shall not be under the necessity of seeking fresh supplies from the cow.

The following observations were obligingly sent me by Mr. Tierny, Assistant Surgeon to the South Gloucester Regiment of Militia, to whom I am indebted for a former report on this subject:

"I inoculated with the cow-pox matter from the eleventh to the latter part of April, twenty-five persons, including women and children. Some on the eleventh were inoculated with the matter Mr. Shrapnell (surgeon to the regiment) had from you, the others with matter taken from these. The progress of the puncture was accurately observed, and its appearance seemed to differ from the smallpox in having less inflammation around its basis on the first days—that is, from the third to the seventh; but after this the inflammation increased, extending on the tenth or eleventh day to a circle of an inch and a half from its centre, and threatening very sore arms; but this I am happy to say was not the case; for, by applying mercurial ointment to the inflamed part, which was repeated daily until the inflammation went off, the arm got well without any further application or trouble. The constitutional symptoms which appeared on the eighth or ninth day after inoculation scarcely deserved the name of disease, as they were so slight as to be scarcely perceptible, except that I could connect a slight headache and languor, with a stiffness and rather painful sensation in the axilla. This latter symptom was the most striking—it remained from twelve to forty-eight hours. In no case did I observe the smallest pustule, or even discolouration of the skin, like an incipient pustule, except about the part where the virus has been applied.

"After all these symptoms had subsided and the arms were well, I inoculated four of this number with variolous matter, taken from a patient in another regiment. In each of these it was inserted several times under the cuticle, producing slight inflammation on the second or third day, and always disappearing before the fifth or sixth, except in one who had the cow-pox in Gloucestershire before he joined us, and who also received it at this time by inoculation. In this man the puncture inflamed and his arm was much sorer than from the insertion of the cow-pox virus; but there was no pain in the axilla, nor could any constitutional affection be observed.

"I have only to add that I am now fully satisfied of the efficacy of the cow-pox in preventing the appearance of the smallpox, and that it is a most happy and salutary substitute for it.   I remain, etc.,

"M. J. TIERNY."

Although the susceptibility of the virus of the cow-pox is, for the most part, lost in those who have had the smallpox, yet in some constitutions it is only partially destroyed, and in others it does not appear to be in the least diminished.

By far the greater number on whom trials were made resisted it entirely; yet I found some on whose arm the pustule from inoculation was formed completely, but without producing the common efflorescent blush around it, or any constitutional illness, while others have had the disease in the most perfect manner. A case of the latter kind having been presented to me by Mr. Fewster, Surgeon, of Thornbury, I shall insert it:

" Three children were inoculated with the vaccine matter you obligingly sent me. On calling to look at their arms three days after I was told that John Hodges, one of the three, had been inoculated with the smallpox when a year old, and that he had a full burthen, of which his face produced plentiful marks, a circumstance I was not before made acquainted with. On the sixth day the arm of the boy appeared as if inoculated with variolous matter, but the pustule was rather more elevated. On the ninth day he complained of violent pain in his head and back, accompanied with vomiting and much fever. The next day he was very well and went to work as usual. The punctured part began to spread, and there was the areola around the inoculated part to a considerable extent.

" As this is contrary to an assertion made in the Medical and Physical Journal, No. 8, I thought it right to give you this information, and remain,

" Dear sir, etc.,

" J. FEWSTER."

It appears, then, that the animal economy with regard to the action of this virus is under the same laws as it is with respect to the variolous virus, after previously feeling its influence, as far as comparisons can be made between the two diseases.

Some striking instances of the power of the cow-pox in

suspending the progress of the smallpox after the patients had been several days casually exposed to the infection have been laid before me by Mr. Lyford, Surgeon, of Winchester, and my nephew, the Rev. G. C. Jenner. Mr. Lyford, after giving an account of his extensive and successful practice in the vaccine inoculation in Hampshire, writes as follows:

"The following case occurred to me a short time since, and may probably be worth your notice. I was sent for to a patient with the smallpox, and on inquiry found that five days previous to my seeing him the eruption began to appear. During the whole of this time two children who had not had the smallpox, were constantly in the room with their father, and frequently on the bed with him. The mother consulted me on the propriety of inoculating them, but objected to my taking the matter from their father, as he was subject to erysipelas. I advised her by all means to have them inoculated at that time, as I could not procure any variolous matter elsewhere. However, they were inoculated with vaccine matter, but I cannot say I flattered myself with its proving successful, as they had previously been so long and still continued to be exposed to the variolous infection. Notwithstanding this I was agreeably surprised to find the vaccine disease advance and go through its regular course; and, if I may be allowed the expression, to the total extinction of the smallpox."

Mr. Jenner's cases were not less satisfactory. He writes as follows:

"A son of Thomas Stinchcomb, of Woodford, near Berkeley, was infected with the natural smallpox at Bristol, and came home to his father's cottage. Four days after the eruptions had appeared upon the boy, the family (none of which had ever had the smallpox), consisting of the father, mother, and five children, was inoculated with vaccine virus. On the arm of the mother it failed to produce the least effect, and she, of course, had the smallpox,[5] but the rest of the family had the cow-pox in the usual way, and were not affected with the smallpox, although they were in the same room, and the children slept in the same bed with their brother

[5] Under similar circumstances I think it would be advisable to insert the matter into each arm, which would be more likely to insure the success of the operation.—E. J.

who was confined to it with the natural smallpox; and subsequently with their mother.

"I attended this family with my brother, Mr. H. Jenner."

The following cases are of too singular a nature to remain unnoticed.

Miss R——, a young lady about five years old, was seized on the evening of the eighth day after inoculation with vaccine virus, with such symptoms as commonly denote the accession of violent fever. Her throat was also a little sore, and there were some uneasy sensations about the muscles of the neck. The day following a rash was perceptible on her face and neck, so much resembling the efflorescence of the *scarlatina anginosa* that I was induced to ask whether Miss R—— had been exposed to the contagion of that disease. An answer in the affirmative, and the rapid spreading of the redness over the skin, at once relieved me from much anxiety respecting the nature of the malady, which went through its course in the ordinary way, but not without symptoms which were alarming both to myself and Mr. Lyford, who attended with me. There was no apparent deviation in the ordinary progress of the pustule to a state of maturity from what we see in general; yet there was a total suspension of the *areola* or florid discolouration around it, until the *scarlatina* had retired from the constitution. As soon as the patient was freed from this disease this appearance advanced in the usual way.[*]

The case of Miss H—— R—— is not less interesting than that of her sister, above related. She was exposed to the contagion of the *scarlatina* at the same time, and sickened almost at the same hour. The symptoms continued severe about twelve hours, when the scarlatina-rash shewed itself faintly upon her face, and partly upon her neck. After remaining two or three hours it suddenly disappeared, and she became perfectly free from every complaint. My surprise at this sudden transition from extreme sickness to health in great measure ceased when I observed that the inoculated pustule had occasioned, in this case, the common efflorescent

[*] I witnessed a similar fact in a case of measles. The pustule from the cow-pock virus advanced to maturity, while the measles existed in the constitution, but no *efflorescence* appeared around it until the measles had ceased to exert its influence.

appearance around it, and that as it approached the centre it was nearly in an erysipelatous state. But the most remarkable part of this history is that, on the fourth day afterwards, so soon as the efflorescence began to die away upon the arm and the pustule to dry up, the *scarlatina* again appeared, her throat became sore, the rash spread all over her. She went fairly through the disease with its common symptoms.

That these were actually cases of *scarlatina* was rendered certain by two servants in the family falling ill at the same time with the distemper, who had been exposed to the infection with the young ladies.

Some there are who suppose the security from the smallpox obtained through the cow-pox will be of a temporary nature only. This supposition is refuted not only by analogy with respect to the habits of diseases of a similar nature, but by incontrovertible facts, which appear in great numbers against it. To those already adduced in the former part of my first treatise[7] many more might be adduced were it deemed necessary; but among the cases I refer to, one will be found of a person who had the cow-pox fifty-three years before the effect of the smallpox was tried upon him. As he completely resisted it, the intervening period I conceive must necessarily satisfy any reasonable mind. Should further evidence be thought necessary, I shall observe that, among the cases presented to me by Mr. Fry, Mr. Darke, Mr. Tierny, Mr. H. Jenner, and others, there were many whom they inoculated ineffectually with variolous matter, who had gone through the cow-pox many years before this trial was made.

It has been imagined that the cow-pox is capable of being communicated from one person to another by effluvia without the intervention of inoculation. My experiments, made with the design of ascertaining this important point, all tend to establish my original position, that it is not infectious except by contact. I have never hesitated to suffer those on whose arms there were pustules exhaling the effluvia from associating or even sleeping with others who never had experienced either the cow-pox or the smallpox. And, further, I have repeatedly, among children, caused the uninfected to breathe

[7] See pages 217, 218, 219, 221, 223, etc.

over the inoculated vaccine pustules during their whole progress, yet these experiments were tried without the least effect.
However, to submit a matter so important to a still further
scrutiny, I desired Mr. H. Jenner to make any further experiments which might strike him as most likely to establish or refute what had been advanced on this subject. He has since
informed me "that he inoculated children at the breast, whose
mothers had not gone through either the smallpox or the
cow-pox; that he had inoculated mothers whose sucking infants had never undergone either of these diseases; that the
effluvia from the inoculated pustules, in either case, had been
inhaled from day to day during the whole progress of their
maturation, and that there was not the least perceptible effect
from these exposures. One woman he inoculated about a
week previous to her *accouchement,* that her infant might
be the more fully and conveniently exposed to the pustule;
but, as in the former instances, no infection was given,
although the child frequently slept on the arm of its mother
with its nostrils and mouth exposed to the pustule in the
fullest state of maturity. In a word, is it not impossible for
the cow-pox, whose *only* manifestation appears to consist in
the pustules *created by contact,* to produce *itself* by effluvia?

In the course of a late inoculation I observed an appearance which it may be proper here to relate. The punctured
part on a boy's arm (who was inoculated with fresh limpid
virus) on the sixth day, instead of shewing a beginning
vesicle, which is usual in the cow-pox at that period, was
encrusted over with a rugged, amber-coloured scab. The
scab continued to spread and increase in thickness for some
days, when, at its edges, a vesicated ring appeared, and the
disease went through its ordinary course, the boy having had
soreness in the axilla and some slight indisposition. With
the fluid matter taken from his arm five persons were inoculated. In one it took no effect. In another it produced a
perfect pustule without any deviation from the common
appearance; but in the other three the progress of the inflammation was exactly similar to the instance which afforded
the virus for their inoculation; there was a creeping scab of
a loose texture, and subsequently the formation of limpid fluid
at its edges. As these people were all employed in laborious

exercises, it is possible that these anomalous appearances might owe their origin to the friction of the clothes on the newly inflamed part of the arm. I have not yet had an opportunity of exposing them to the smallpox.

In the early part of this inquiry I felt far more anxious respecting the inflammation of the inoculated arm than at present; yet that this affection will go on to a greater extent than could be wished is a circumstance sometimes to be expected. As this can be checked, or even entirely subdued, by very simple means, I see no reason why the patient should feel an uneasy hour because an application may not be absolutely necessary. About the tenth or eleventh day, if the pustule has proceeded regularly, the appearance of the arm will almost to a certainty indicate whether this is to be expected or not. Should it happen, nothing more need be done than to apply a single drop of the *aqua lythargyri acetati*[8] upon the pustule, and, having suffered it to remain two or three minutes, to cover the efflorescence surrounding the pustule with a piece of linen dipped in the *aqua lythargyri compos.*[9] The former may be repeated twice or thrice during the day, the latter as often as it may feel agreeable to the patient.

When the scab is prematurely rubbed off (a circumstance not unfrequent among children and working people), the application of a little *aqua lythargyri acet.* to the part immediately coagulates the surface, which supplies its place, and prevents a sore.

In my former treatises on this subject I have remarked that the human constitution frequently retains its susceptibility to the smallpox contagion (both from effluvia and contact) after previously feeling its influence. In further corroboration of this declaration many facts have been communicated to me by various correspondents. I shall select one of them.

"DEAR SIR:

"Society at large must, I think, feel much indebted to you for your Inquiries and Observations on the Nature and Effects of the Variolæ Vaccinæ, etc., etc. As I conceive

[8] Extract of Saturn.
[9] Goulard water. For further information on this subject see the first Treatise on the Var. Vac., Dr. Marshall's letters, etc.

what I am now about to communicate to be of some importance, I imagine it cannot be uninteresting to you, especially as it will serve to corroborate your assertion of the susceptibility of the human system of the variolous contagion, although it has previously been made sensible of its action. In November, 1793, I was desired to inoculate a person with the smallpox. I took the variolous matter from a child under the disease in the natural way, who had a large burthen of distinct pustules. The mother of the child being desirous of seeing my method of communicating the disease by inoculation, after having opened a pustule, I introduced the point of my lancet in the usual way on the back part of my own hand, and thought no more of it until I felt a sensation in the part which reminded me of the transaction. This happened upon the third day; on the fourth there were all the appearances common to inoculation, at which I was not at all surprised, nor did I feel myself uneasy upon perceiving the inflammation continue to increase to the sixth and seventh day, accompanied with a very small quantity of fluid, repeated experiments having taught me it might happen so with persons who had undergone the disease, and yet would escape any constitutional affection; but I was not so fortunate; for on the eighth day I was seized with all the symptoms of the eruptive fever, but in a much more violent degree than when I was before inoculated, which was about eighteen years previous to this, when I had a considerable number of pustules. I must confess I was now greatly alarmed, although I had been much engaged in the smallpox, having at different times inoculated not less than two thousand persons. I was convinced my present indisposition proceeded from the insertion of the variolous matter, and, therefore, anxiously looked for an eruption. On the tenth day I felt a very unpleasant sensation of stillness and heat on each side of my face near my ear, and the fever began to decline. The affection in my face soon terminated in three or four pustules attended with inflammation, but which did not maturate, and I was presently well.

"I remain, dear sir, etc.,

"THOMAS MILES."

This inquiry is not now so much in its infancy as to restrain me from speaking more positively than formerly on the important point of scrophula as connected with the smallpox.

Every practitioner in medicine who has extensively inoculated with the smallpox, or has attended many of those who have had the distemper in the natural way, must acknowledge that he has frequently seen scrophulous affections, in some form or another, sometimes rather quickly shewing themselves after the recovery of the patients. Conceiving this fact to be admitted, as I presume it must be by all who have carefully attended to the subject, may I not ask whether it does not appear probable that the general introduction of the smallpox into Europe has not been among the most conductive means in exciting that formidable foe to health? Having attentively watched the effects of the cow-pox in this respect, I am happy in being able to declare that the disease does not appear to have the least tendency to produce this destructive malady.

The scepticism that appeared, even among the most enlightened of medical men when my sentiments on the important subject of the cow-pox were first promulgated, was highly laudable. To have admitted the truth of a doctrine, at once so novel and so unlike any thing that ever had appeared in the annals of medicine, without the test of the most rigid scrutiny, would have bordered upon temerity; but now, when that scrutiny has taken place, not only among ourselves, but in the first professional circles in Europe, and when it has been uniformly found in such abundant instances that the human frame, when once it has felt the influence of the genuine cow-pox in the way that has been described, is never afterwards at any period of its existence assailable by the smallpox, may I not with perfect confidence congratulate my country and society at large on their beholding, in the mild form of the cow-pox, an antidote that is capable of extirpating from the earth a disease which is every hour devouring its victims; a disease that has ever been considered as the severest scourge of the human race!

www.ingramcontent.com/pod-product-compliance
Lightning Source LLC
LaVergne TN
LVHW091941060326
832903LV00043B/10

* 9 7 8 1 1 6 1 5 9 5 8 5 7 *